domestic
violence
survival
guide

BY Cliff Mariani

EDITED BY Patricia Sokolich

LOOSELEAF LAW PUBLICATIONS, INC

I. S. B. N. 0-930137-99-X

**LOOSELEAF LAW
PUBLICATIONS, INC.**
41-23 150th Street, Flushing, New York 11355
(718) 359-5559 *also* FAX (718) 539-0941

Domestic Violence

SURVIVAL GUIDE

Written
by
Cliff Mariani

New York City Police Department
(Retired)
New York, NY

■

Associate Editor,
Looseleaf Law Publications, Inc.
Flushing, NY

■

Member, New York State Coalition
Against Domestic Violence
Albany, NY

i

About the Author

DOMESTIC VIOLENCE SURVIVAL GUIDE

For over 25 years, Cliff Mariani was a member of the New York City Police Department. As a patrol officer, he had more than frequent occasion to deal with domestic abusers, their victims and the "system" which is expected to work on their behalf.

Cliff began his writing career in the early 1970's. With an eye for detail and a skill with words, he wrote unique and innovative study and reference publications for the law enforcement community.

Catching the attention of the Director of Modern Promotion Courses, Inc., of Flushing, N.Y., Cliff signed on as an assistant editor. In that capacity, he reviewed and updated all legal and topical materials that required amending or other necessary revisions.

Currently, as a research writer and consultant to Looseleaf Law Publications, Inc., he combines his law enforcement, publishing and administrative background with his creative talents, to write and edit numerous reference guides and study manuals for the law enforcement and criminal justice communities.

Domestic Violence

SURVIVAL GUIDE

Edited
by
Patricia A. Sokolich

Attorney at Law
Matrimonial Law & Women's Issues
Garden City, NY

■

Co-President,
Queens Women's Center
Queens County, NY

■

Founder and Director,
Q. W. C. Legal Clinic for
Women in Crisis

DOMESTIC VIOLENCE SURVIVAL GUIDE

Patricia Sokolich lends an area of expertise to this publication which is invaluable. A graduate of City University at Queens College Law School, Ms. Sokolich was, until recently, affiliated with the prestigious law firm of Leavitt, Kerson & Leffler. At present, she is in private practice in Garden City, Long Island, N.Y., specializing in matrimonial law and women's issues.

With a Master's Degree in Library Science, Pat uses her research and investigative skills on a daily basis to facilitate her professional commitments and better serve her client's needs.

Having a deep commitment to the cause of women's rights, Pat enjoys the hands-on experience of working with battered and abused women. Not surprisingly, she is Co-President of the Queens Women's Center....a voluntary, non-profit, non-partisan organization, which exists solely on volunteer help.

Strongly believing that women's stories need to be told in order to dispel the shame associated with matrimonial abuse and to provide these women with access to the legal system, Pat is also the Founder and Director of the Q.W.C. Legal Clinic for Women in Crisis.

A frequent guest speaker at forums and seminars, Pat graciously shares her knowledge and experience on domestic violence with her listeners, and now with our readers.

Domestic Violence

SURVIVAL GUIDE

Published
by
Looseleaf Law Publications, Inc.

Proudly Serving the
Law Enforcement, Criminal Justice,
Legal & Educational Communities
for Over Three Decades

■

Business Office:
41-23 150th Street
Flushing, NY 11355
Tel. 718 / 359-5559

■

Mailing Address:
P.O. Box 650042
Fresh Meadows, NY 11365
24 Hour Fax 718 / 539-0941

About the Publisher

DOMESTIC VIOLENCE SURVIVAL GUIDE

For over three decades, Looseleaf Law Publications has been serving the New York - New Jersey - Connecticut region with quality law books and study aids for the law enforcement, criminal justice, educational and private sector.

Founded in 1964 by retired N.Y.C. Police Captain William J. McCullough, Looseleaf Law Publications continues today with a tradition of innovation, accuracy and fair pricing.

Always on the lookout for topics of special interest and concern to our customers and subscribers, we are proud to add the Domestic Violence Survival Guide to our ever-expanding catalog of fine publications.

DOMESTIC VIOLENCE SURVIVAL GUIDE

The immense effort and energy expended to produce this publication, from inception to completion, is hereby dedicated to the **victims** of all ages, races, regions, religions, nationalities and backgrounds, who have *suffered* at the hands of a relationship abuser or violent partner.

Recognition is extended to those dedicated persons, be they paid professionals or unpaid volunteers, whether from public agencies or private organizations, who *intervene* on behalf of those victims: the health and medical personnel, social workers and victim's advocates, shelter administrators and staff members, law counselors and criminal justice employees.

Not to be overlooked are the men and women of our police and sheriff's departments who are frequently injured and killed while rendering aid and assistance to the victims of domestic violence.

All persons who go above and beyond the call of duty in an effort to make our communities a better, safer place, deserve our appreciation, admiration and respect.

May they always be there....ready, willing and able to help the victims in the **survival** process.

Table of Contents

DOMESTIC VIOLENCE SURVIVAL GUIDE

Preface

DOMESTIC VIOLENCE SURVIVAL GUIDE

Ideally, domestic violence should be **recognized** early in the relationship, then **prevented** before it erupts.

If it cannot be prevented, it must be **stopped** before serious harm is done.

If it cannot be stopped, the victim must be **protected** before further harm is done.

Once the victim is protected, she must be **rehabilitated** to become a whole person once again.

But **how** do we accomplish these goals in a safe, sane, practical and legal way? And can the abuser be helped? Is reconciliation ever possible? That is the theme of this publication.

Based on a review and analysis of pertinent studies, surveys, reports and findings of various public and private agencies and advocacy groups, the author has incorporated his first-hand knowledge and experience as a former law enforcement officer and research writer to produce a uniquely designed self-help book of special interest to:

- Victims and family members.
- The law enforcement community.
- Criminal justice system personnel.
- Laymen, para-professionals and students.
- All persons directly and indirectly affected by domestic violence.

Introduction

DOMESTIC VIOLENCE SURVIVAL GUIDE

I was pleased and honored to be selected as editor of the Domestic Violence Survival Guide. As an attorney and an advocate to victims of domestic violence, I have long been aware of the acute need for a volume such as this. While there is a plethora of information available on the subject, no one has compiled the information into a user-friendly volume that explains the "how to" of domestic violence.

The author has filled a unique gap in the literature by providing the professional, the lay volunteer and the victims themselves with a unique "self-help" guide that not only provides the history and rationale of domestic abuse, but lists key characteristics to help the would be victim recognize and avoid a potential abuser. His lists of "Preventive Measures," "Survival Tips," "Protecting Your Children," and his "Evacuation Pack," are sure to empower and give hope to all victims of Domestic Violence.

Domestic Violence is a universal problem that cuts across every class and race in our society. It is not defined by culture, age, education or economics. Domestic Violence occurs in relationships between couples currently dating, couples who have dated; unmarried people who are living together; gay or lesbian couples; married couples; former spouses; and in many cases it involves the children of the above mentioned relationships.

It is time that professionals, counselors, volunteers, human resource people and the victims themselves, uncover the shocking details of family violence. In studying this problem, experts have found that there is no "classic profile" that helps to identify the "batterer" or the "victim." Experts have found that the most common thread that runs through the lives of both "batterers" and "victims" is that they have learned their role through modeling. They have either seen violence in their parent's relationship or they have themselves been the victims of family violence. In any event, the only way to address the problem is to strip it of the shame that has long been associated with Domestic Violence.

Cliff has compiled an enormous amount of material, into an easy to use compendium of information that is available to both the professional counselor, the volunteer who answers the Hot Line at your local shelter, and more importantly, the victim herself. His easy to read and graphically appealing style provide a source of information and a basis for understanding anyone who is involved with an abuser or is a victim of abuse.

Mr. Mariani should be commended for his excellent work on behalf of victims everywhere. We need more male voices to rise up and uncover this insidious giant that devours family life and destroys relationships. Too long has it been hidden under a blanket of shame, knitted together by the many fears that face the victims of Domestic Violence.

Patricia A. Sokolich, Esq.
Garden City, New York

Chapter One

RELATIONSHIPS

This page intentionally left blank.

Part 1- A

ORIENTATION

We now begin our exploration of domestic violence with a concise background examination. Before attempting to survive a bout with this national affliction, we must learn as much as we can about the subject.

DOMESTIC VIOLENCE EXAMINED

Literally speaking, domestic violence pertains to a *violent* act or acts which take place primarily in the home between a (current or former) spouse, lover, boy/girl friend, live-in, etc. The abused-abuser are *usually* of the opposite sex but *may* also be of the same sex.

For purposes of our discussion, the term "Domestic Violence" shall denote activities or behavior of a physically aggressive and criminal nature which have, may or will result in death or serious bodily harm.

Although the residence is the *usual* place of occurrence, domestic violence can take place at the home of another person (family, friend or neighbor), the victim's place of employment, a store, a commercial establishment or in public.

UNDERSTANDING DOMESTIC VIOLENCE

Domestic violence is a problem of epidemic proportions with far-reaching *consequences* for the victim, their loved ones and the community. As a highly effective means of *control,* the recipient (of such violence) and the target (of such control) will expend a great deal of energy trying to avoid subsequent assaults. These endeavors usually include attempts to anticipate the needs, wishes and whims of the partner.

In effect, domestic violence is a menace to the safety and sanctuary of the home and a scourge upon the family....crippling and destroying the concept of a loving and nurturing environment.

Domestic violence is not a private, family matter. It is a **criminal** offense which tends to repeat itself, leads to other crimes and turns child abuse victims into future adult victims and abusers themselves.

Presently, the cost to society is enormous and still rising. Social, legal, medical and criminal justice services bear the brunt of the economic assault upon the taxpayer.

Domestic violence, often has more complex causes and solutions than crimes committed by unknown assailants (i.e., purse snatchers, muggers, car thieves, burglars, etc.). For those whose lives have never been touched by domestic violence, it can be difficult to understand and nearly impossible to empathize with.

No one deserves to be abused and no one has a "right" to abuse another. Since violence is a learned behavior which *can* be reversed, there is *hope* for the victim, the family and society.

ORIGINS OF ABUSE

For centuries, men were legally and socially permitted to *chastise* their wives. What we now call spousal abuse or domestic violence was once considered a *legitimate* means by which men could maintain supreme control of their families.

A wife's disobedience or a child's disloyalty brought about *consequences*. Evidence of abuse was evidence of having been made to face those consequences.

This once accepted method of maintaining control within the household was considered necessary for a smooth running society. "Prerogative" was freely resorted to lest the man meet with social disapproval for not applying the expected level of discipline, up to and including beating his wife and children, if necessary.

As laws were written to provide guidelines for social order, "disciplining" activities occurring within the home were omitted because such "private, family-related" behavior was expected and accepted. But as wives and children eventually ceased to be viewed as the equivalent of property, laws emerged to proscribe such behavior.

No longer customary and acceptable from a social and legal standpoint, husbands and fathers may not treat their women and children as chattel and keep them under control through battering.

Unfortunately, domestic violence is still not quite out of the shadows of social precedents and cultural preconceptions. The "prerogative issue" is blurred with attitudes and assumptions by most of those who batter and many of those who deal with the batterer and victim, after the fact.

AWARENESS

With an eye focused on better understanding domestic violence, we continue on the learning path toward an awakening process.

BATTERING AND ABUSE DEFINED

Battering is a consistent pattern *of behavior* ....that seeks to establish *dominance, power and control* over another.... through fear, intimidation and the threat of or actual use of....physical, psychological, sexual or economic abuse.... and often escalates to the use of violence.

The term "battering" used herein shall generally imply the assaultive use of *force* with the *potential* to cause or in fact to result in physical *injury*. Examples include pulling hair, punching, kicking, beating and other forms of harmful *physical* contact.

The term "abuse" shall encompass behavior which is *less* physical but *more* psychological or economic in nature. Examples include ridiculing, name-calling, yelling, threatening, intimidating, spying and various other types of harassing or controlling behavior.

Note that violence and battering constitute abuse but not all abuse constitutes battering or violence.

These are broad-based *behavioral* definitions as opposed to narrow, *legal* definitions.

Domestic violence is frequently a *repeated* condition, rather than a one-time occurrence. Even after a lull, the victim is seldom truly safe. Once violence manifests itself, there is a constant, lingering likelihood that it will reoccur at the slightest "provocation."

BATTERER'S BELIEF

Battering occurs when the abuser *believes* that he/she is *entitled to control* their partner, the abused being the "property" of the abuser. Furthermore, the abuser believes that violence is *acceptable and productive.*

SIDE EFFECTS

Domestic violence causes death, serious injury, physical pain and mental impairment to *both* abuser and abused, as well as those directly and indirectly involved in the abusive relationship, such as children, family, friends, co-workers and intervention personnel.

Anxiety, depression, emotional problems, drug/alcohol/medication abuse, suicidal tendencies, financial instability, family fallout, separation or divorce, employment or residential relocation and homelessness are frequent by-products of domestic abuse.

VICTIMS

Victims come in many varieties and from all walks of life:

■ **Women** - numerically, suffer a higher percentage of abuse cases.

■ **Men** - less publicized and to a significantly lesser degree than women, but must not be overlooked.

■ **Children** - living in a violent home usually results in abuse, maltreatment or neglect.

■ **Family Structure** - all persons living within the abuser's home are subject to dysfunction.

■ **Elderly** - are often an easy target to be abused or neglected by their adult children or caretakers.

■ **Unborn** - often suffer in the womb by direct or indirect attack upon the mother's physical health or emotional well-being.

DEMOGRAPHICS

In varying degrees, domestic violence occurs among all segments of society: racial, ethnic and religious; educational, professional and occupational; economic and geographical; age group and gender; homosexual and heterosexual. Though all these assorted segments contribute to the problem, battering among lower income or disadvantaged socioeconomic groups is more likely to come to the attention of public agencies, therefore, their numbers may seem disproportionately higher.

REPORTING

Incidents of domestic violence are believed to be significantly under-reported and misdiagnosed. This factor, coupled with *known* cases on record, reveals a much *larger* problem for society.

Reasons for not reporting a domestic incident include:

1. A tendency to downplay the incident.

2. A hesitancy to make public, a "private, personal" matter.

3. A reluctance to criminalize a "family" matter.

4. An inability to adequately articulate abuse which is not physically apparent.

5. Lack of faith in the "system."

6. Fear of reprisal.

STATS

Statistics can be dull and boring, but they can drive home a point. In this case, the point is that domestic violence is Excessive, Pervasive, Destructive, Costly and Debilitating.

On the bright side however, it can be *contained* and ultimately *reduced* through effective counseling and support programs, a conscientious law enforcement effort and a well coordinated follow-through by the criminal justice system.

FACTS & FIGURES

⌂ Domestic violence is believed to be the *most* common yet *least* reported crime in the country.

⌂ The full magnitude of the problem may never be realized due to the *non-reporting* and *under-reporting* of abusive incidents.

⌂ Even the most reliable statistics (i.e., F.B.I. Reports) are an inaccurate reflection of what is *really* taking place in American homes.

⌂ It is safe to speculate however, that domestic abuse is *more prevalent* than we realize.

⌂ An estimated 6 million American women are beaten each year by their male partners.

⌂ Over 4,000 women are *killed* as a result of domestic violence each year.

⌂ A female is more likely to be assaulted, injured, raped or killed by a male partner than by *any other* type of assailant.

⌂ Wife-beating results in *more injuries* requiring medical treatment than rape, auto accidents and muggings *combined.*

⌂ Approximately 50% of all marriages experience *at least one episode* of domestic violence.

⌂ Approximately 20% of all marriages experience *on-going* episodes of domestic violence (5 or more incidents per year).

⌂ Once victimized, the chances are *high* of being victimized again.

⌂ Pregnancy or disability is *not* a deterrent to being victimized; pregnancy often triggers the first assault from an *insecure* partner who feels *threatened* by the "intruder."

⌂ The chances of *miscarriage* are high in such battered women.

⌂ Many men who abuse their partners, also abuse their *children/step-children.*

⌂ Children from abusive homes have an increased propensity to *perpetuate* the cycle of violence as *adults.*

DYNAMICS OF ABUSE

Domestic abuse has many facets and characteristics to explore.

LEVELS OF ABUSE

Abuse has at least three tentacles with which to swat and harm its victims:

❶   NON-PHYSICAL LEVEL - yelling, screaming, cursing, threatening language; *tension* builds.

❷   PHYSICAL LEVEL - pushing, shoving, slapping, assaulting; *fear* ensues.

❸   EMOTIONAL LEVEL - apologies, expressions of regret, promises to change; *confusion* sets in.

FORMS OF BATTERING

Batterers can employ a variety of tactics, some patently unlawful, some not. Episodes can be frequent or sporadic, sometimes without warning, sometimes not.

In addition to outright physical abuse, battering can include Verbal Abuse, Emotional Abuse, Mental Abuse, Economic Abuse, Sexual Abuse and Child Abuse or any variation of, or combination of the above, used against the partner to instill *fear* and establish *power.*

ESCALATION OF BATTERING

The batterer plots his course and sets his "limits" in the early stages of the relationship:

- "I'll yell a lot so she knows what I expect *but* I won't slap her around."

- "I'll blow off steam once in a while *but* I'd never punch her out."

- "I'll have to hit her so she knows I'm in charge *but* I won't hurt her."

- "I'll have to hurt her this time to make her do what I want *but* I'd never beat her up."

- "She needs to know it's my way or no way *but* I'd never kill her."

Not all yellers are potential batterers *but* verbal attacks can be the *first* step toward physical abuse. The pre-set "limits" of domestic dominance are often violated, thus escalation begins. New and higher limits are set, then abuse turns to violence.

Battering may *begin* with name-calling, banging an inanimate object or kicking the dog. Next might come pushing or slapping; then punching or striking; then choking, beating or other life-threatening assaults. Ultimately, battering can and does lead to murder/manslaughter.

CYCLE OF VIOLENCE

Phase One - Escalation; a period of increasing stress and tension; usually brought about as a result of coercive tactics used to *control* the victim. The effectiveness of these tactics depend, at least in part, on the batterer's ability to instill *fear* in the victim.

Phase Two - Acute Battering Incident; typically characterized as a physical assault, yet other forms of abuse can be equally effective in reinforcing the batterer's power and control (i.e., displaying a weapon, threatening harm to children, etc.) The incidents often bring about a 911 call for emergency assistance. If Phase Three kicks in quickly enough, the call for police assistance may be averted.

Phase Three - De-escalation; a return to a period of calm, accompanied by contriteness; this phase allows the abuser to seek forgiveness, express remorse and profess an intense or renewed commitment to the relationship. This false sense of hope may cause the victim to back away from the notion of pursuing criminal charges.

Phase Four - Repetition; note that the symptoms displayed in Phase One may aid health care professionals to identify domestic abuse victims and institute support services....an intense show of force in Phase Two and the ongoing threat of its repetition, are the primary mechanisms used to instill fear and preview resistance. Just knowing the batterer's potential and willingness to use violence becomes the controlling force in attaining and maintaining maximum control....not all batterer's engage in Phase Three, which is not to be confused with non-abusive behavior or an end of abuse. Instead, de-escalation represents a different form of abuse, a manipulation of the victim's emotions.

FUEL TO PROPEL THE CYCLE

The cycle of violence is propelled by the human emotions of:

■ **Love** -   of the partner.

■ **Hope** -   for change and improvement.

■ **Fear** -   of consequences if the victim attempts to leave.

Because these ingredients are often in abundant supply and likewise difficult to control, the potential for out-of-control propulsion of the cycle is not hard to understand.

FORMULA FOR MORE OF THE SAME $+ / =$

Historical Precedent
+ Machismo Tendencies
+ Objectification of Women
+ Glorification of Violence
+ Media Exploitation of Women
+ Oppressive Attitudes
+ Sexism, Racism and Classism
+ Indifferent Public
+ Victim-Blaming Mentality
+ Inadequate Social Services
+ Women's Economic Inequality
+ Difficulty in Obtaining Protection Orders
+ Inadequate Prosecution
+ Lack of Criminal Sanctions
+ Victim's Defeatist Attitudes
+ Lack of Accountability
+ Absence of Consequences
+ Untreated Behavioral Disorders

= **Continuation of the Problem**

This page intentionally left blank.

Part 1 - B

RECOGNITION

|F| or our purposes, there are essentially two types of relationships: new (or relatively new) and established (or on-going).

This chapter will therefore be divided into two segments as we explore the topic of recognition; discovering how to recognize (and thereby avoid) an abuser in a *new* relationship and recognize (and hopefully leave) an abuser in an *established* relationship.

NEW RELATIONSHIPS

Each relationship begins with an attraction, some attention, then affection. Each union has its own origins, its own components, its own history, its own aura and its own uniqueness.

Hazard or warning signals however, can be universally applied to *any* relationship.

This section provides three categories of "Hazard Signals" to aid in the Recognition process:

1 **WARNING SIGNS:** which are relatively easy to spot in a new relationship and are not necessarily serious character flaws in and of themselves.

2 **CAUTION SIGNS:** which are progressively more detrimental to a compatible relationship and should indicate a definite problem, especially when discovered in quantity.

3 **DANGER SIGNS:** which indicate trouble, plain and simple.

WARNING SIGNS !

The following list of tell-tale indicators should *assist* you in predicting whether or not a NEW social acquaintance or dating partner *is* or *could be* a potential abuser. The *more* negative traits discovered, the more *likely* the person is an abuser.

❑ **Quick Involvement** - comes on very strong; seems anxious to solidify the relationship.

❑ **Inconsistent -** says one thing and does another....often, and at your expense.

❑ **Manipulative** - "sweet-talks" you into doing things you would prefer not to do and dissuades you from doing things you wish to do.

❑ **Loner** - prefers that you do not meet his family, friends (if any) or co-workers.

❑ **Argumentative** - can't seem to agree on anything; appears to enjoy constant confrontation.

❑ **Hypersensitive** - seems easily insulted; feelings are hurt on a frequent basis; constantly complaining.

❑ **Blames Others** - other people are the cause of his problems and setbacks, his feelings and emotions.

CAUTION SIGNS ! !

❏ **Isolator** - would like to cut you off from your family and friends (whom he "dislikes") and suggests that you quit your job and social organizations if the relationship is to continue.

❏ **Jealous / Possessive** - checks up on you out of "concern" but in reallty does not trust you; makes unfounded accusations; interrogates you to satisfy his groundless suspicions.

❏ **Control Freak** - attempts to question and control your activities, decisions, purchases, personal and social affairs out of "concern" for your safety and well-being.

❏ **Verbal Abuse** - makes cruel, hurtful, degrading assessments of others; constantly criticizes.

❏ **Unrealistic Expectations** - expects perfection in all things and full compliance with his wishes.

❏ **Sexist Attitude** - views women as inferior beings who should remain at home in subservient roles.

❏ **Sudden Mood Swings** - reveals "Jekyll & Hyde" personality traits; sweet one minute, explodes the next, without provocation.

❏ **"Short Fuse"** - hot tempered, "fly off the handle" reaction when things go wrong.

❏ **Cruel To Others** - shows unrealistic expectations re: young child's abilities or potential; teases or punishes a child without cause; exhibits cruelty to animals; insensitive to pain and suffering of others.

❏ **"Playful" / Forceful Sex** - enjoys "rough stuff" and finds the idea of rape exciting; reveals selfish and demanding sex habits.

DANGER SIGNS ! ! !

❑ **Argues With Force** - uses unnecessary and excessive force during an argument; holds you down, physically restrains, punches, shoves, pinches, etc. Forces you to "listen" to him.

❑ **Threats Of Violence** - makes threatening statements such as "I'll break your neck" or "I'll kill you" then dismisses statements as "just talk."

❑ **Breaks / Strikes Objects** - beats on table or counter top with fists; throws objects at, near or around his partner; displays emotional immaturity by breaking prized possessions as a means of punishment and to terrorize you into submission.

❑ **Past Battering** - admits to hitting women in the past but claims they made him do it; past victims alert you to his history; claims he'd never hit you because he "loves" you.

SET YOUR ANTENNA

Your first few dates with Mr. Prospective are to get *acquainted* and to gather *information.* Extending the benefit of any doubts about him may be the polite and sometimes necessary way to go but *doubt* is in itself a red flag and must be *resolved.*

Expect a degree of nervousness from the *average* male. Like yourself, he wants to look his best and impress his date. But if his "best" is later found to be fraught with personality and character flaws *beyond* redemption, call it quits fast. You *don't* need this guy.

To help get a "reading" on your tentative selection, make a *list* of any troubling violations of impropriety and *contrast* it against a list of positive attributes. But remember: a person's good points are usually subject to *verification* but their "bad" points can generally be taken a face value.

The bottom line will be, is he a real bargain, or a bogus parcel of heartache?

DOING YOUR PART

In order for a relationship to get into gear, there must be good *communication* based upon openness and honesty. Expressing your *true* feelings is the first step in formulating the necessary degree of honesty. In the communication process, *mutuality* of effort is essential for success. The longer one or both parties takes to *express* themselves, the longer it will take for them to truly *discover* each other.

How your communication is *received* can be a *warning* indicator in itself. Negative responses such as anger, indignation, withdrawal, etc. cast a negative reflection upon the recipient of such communication.

FALSE OR CONFUSING SIGNALS ???

He may *remind* you of an unpleasant partner from the past. It could be just the shape of his nose or the way he slurps his soup. Or, you may be picking up signals.... subtle or subliminal messages transmitted through his mannerisms, his vocal inflections or the content of his conversations.

Working *against* you can be preconceived notions based upon sketchy biographical data which can mislead and disappoint.

Also, the presence of drugs, alcohol, nicotine and caffeine can *distort* one's perception about the person in your presence.

To compound the problems for some women, the psychological impetus to marry, whether to satisfy family expectations, cultural dictates or an advancing biological clock, can put powerful and destructive pressure upon the woman to "land a catch" ....regardless of the consequences.

JUST FRIENDS !   ? OK ?

If you have stated that you *just* want to be friends and he agrees....albeit reluctantly....to date you under those conditions, be *alert* to statements and gestures which run *contrary* to a "just friends" relationship, such as: excessive phone calls, impertinent questions, unreasonable demands, expensive gifts or indications of jealousy, possessiveness or controlling tactics.

CALLING IT QUITS

You've been dating Mr. Maybe for a few weeks now. You've seen *some* minor problems and a few *potentially* major ones. Whether you stay on his carousel or jump off, depends upon what you're *looking* for in a relationship *and* your level of *tolerance.*

As your new relationship progresses, step back and take a *personal* assessment. Above all, be *honest* with yourself. Determine how you *feel*. Does he make you feel good, bad or indifferent? Do you feel like an *equal* partner in the relationship or an insignificant player on his roster of conquests?

Does he make you happy and upbeat....or does he bring you down and out of sorts? Does he *truly* light up your life....or does he darken your doorstep with shadows of suspicion and doubt?

Ask yourself, will I accept 10 plus points offset by 5 minus points or must there be no more than 2 minus points scored against Mr. Maybe? Are you flexible....and if so, to what degree? Is he *capable* of mending minor bad habits....and if so, is change *likely* to occur?

Communicating your concerns early on, in terms of your personal feelings....how his *behavior* makes you *feel*....may help to resolve minor problems. If he reveals *major* problems, remember that you are *not* his mother or his therapist.

TELLTALE INDICATORS

In addition to or in conjunction with the basic warning signs which you just reviewed....and in the *absence* of legitimate reason, some extraordinary circumstances or an occasional bad mood....does your new acquaintance do any of the following:

☐ He is always late, but never without an "excuse."

☐ He has stood you up more than once.

☐ He has shown up at your door while *intoxicated.*

☐ He has trouble keeping his word.

☐ He often has two versions of the truth.

☐ He seems "different" on each date.

☐ He can only see you on say, Tuesday nights.

☐ He seems to lead two different lives.

☐ Though *not* a hunter, he avidly collects all sorts of weapons.

☐ He's *anxious* to show you his collection of sex toys and bondage paraphernalia.

☐ His fantasies are scary to you.

☐ He seems to have a *sadistic* streak.

☐ His values are significantly *different* from yours.

☐ He is *very* judgmental.

☐ He has very pronounced *racist* views.

☐ His *integrity* level seems low.

☐ He has a poor *work* ethic.

☐ He thinks society *owes* him a living.

☐ He wants everything *now!*

☐ He is very inquisitive about your personal and/or family *assets.*

☐ He repeatedly changes the subject if you ask too many personal questions.

☐ He shuts off his answering machine and avoids checking his messages when you go to his place for a drink.

☐ He seems superficial.

☐ He shows a lack of interest and/or respect for his mother, sister, ex-wife, children, etc.

☐ He doesn't think very much of women in general.

☐ He keeps checking out all the other women wherever you go.

☐ He lays out his ground rules for a "successful" relationship.

☐ He likes to be in charge on the date.

☐ He boasts about how he put his past partners "in their place."

☐ He *challenges* the veracity of your statements.

☐ He doesn't seem to be interested in what *you* have to say.

☐ He tends to *minimize* your input.

☐ He finds it necessary to "correct" you often.

☐ He gets easily agitated by your comments.

☐ He seems to bristle when you *disagree* with him.

☐ He gets irritated if you fail to follow his "suggestions."

☐ He has poor *coping* mechanisms.

☐ He gets frustrated *very* easily.

☐ He seems *angry* quite often.

☐ He tends to make mountains out of mole hills.

☐ He gets mean sometimes, but not without "good reason."

☐ He seems to lack *basic* manners.

☐ He can't seem to loosen up until he drinks.

☐ His *friends* are loud, rowdy and obnoxious.

☐ His "best" friend is a creep.

☐ His driving is reckless and irresponsible and demonstrates a distinct level of *immaturity.*

☐ He seems edgy and nervous.

☐ He makes you feel edgy and uncomfortable.

ESTABLISHED RELATIONSHIPS

This section provides two important areas to examine:

1) Characteristics of an **Abuser**
-and-
2) Characteristics of a **Victim**

Utilize the checklist to help determine if your partner is an **abuser** and/or if you are a **victim**.

THE ABUSER

With an emphasis on Power and Control, how many of the following characteristics of an *abuser* apply to *your* partner?

◘ **ISOLATES** - controls who you see, speak with; regulates activity, even phone calls and reading material; limits or prevents all outside involvement....social, educational, occupational, etc.

◘ **EMOTIONS** - plays constant head games; frequently engages in name-calling and put-downs; utilizes degradation and humiliation; attempts to create guilt, and foster poor self-image, threatens to harm himself or others.

◘ **SEXISM** - defines roles, treats you like a servant, makes all the big decisions, rules his domain his way.

◘ **SEXUAL** - dictates sexual policy (i.e., where, when how, etc.) critiques, withholds, demands, treats you in demeaning and inconsiderate manner.

◘ **INTIMIDATES** - instills fear by facial expression, gesture, body language, display of weapon; bangs, smashes, destroys items of value; abuses pets.

◼ **THREATENS** - makes or carries out threats to cause harm, kill; threatens to leave, commit suicide, report on partner (i.e., to I.R.S., Welfare Dept., etc.).

◼ **PHYSICAL** - subjects you to physical injury and/ or illness; withholds resources and/or access to medical needs.

◼ **FINANCES** - demands financial accountability; seeks total control over financial resources; prevents getting/keeping a job; puts you on an allowance; punishes via purse strings; promotes need to beg for money.

◼ **CHILDREN** - children become pawns to relay mess-ages, generate rivalry between parents and siblings, provide opportunity to harass you during visitation; he may threaten to abduct them or allege their abuse at your hands.

◼ **COERCES** - partner to drop charges or perform an illegal act or activity.

◼ **COMPOUNDS ABUSE** - makes situation worse by minimizing or outright denying abusive/violent ways; shifts blame for all household problems onto you; makes light of your fears, concerns and injuries.

ABUSER'S PERSONAL BEHAVIOR TRAITS

☐ Looses self-control easily (and often).
☐ Punches anything in his proximity when angry.
☐ Has explosive temper.
☐ Handles frustration and stress poorly.

- ☐ Uses profanity regardless of who's around.
- ☐ Is emotionally unpredictable.
- ☐ Acts "strange" every so often.
- ☐ Is often depressed.
- ☐ Pouts and sulks at the least little thing.
- ☐ Is very impatient.
- ☐ Wants it his way or no way.
- ☐ Is unwilling to compromise.
- ☐ Always takes, seldom gives.
- ☐ Is very "now" minded.
- ☐ Has low self-esteem.
- ☐ Feels unsuccessful.
- ☐ Believes he has poor social skills.
- ☐ Is outwardly charming but socially withdrawn.
- ☐ Is often insecure.
- ☐ Unable to handle rejection or criticism.
- ☐ Has difficulty expressing his feelings.
- ☐ Usually blames others for all difficulties and faults.
- ☐ Has become impotent.
- ☐ Shows signs of incestuous inclinations.
- ☐ Was physically or sexually abused as a child.
- ☐ Grew up in a violent home.

ABUSER'S TRAITS AFFECTING THE RELATIONSHIP

- ☐ States relationship with you is closest he's *ever* known.
- ☐ Is emotionally *dependent* upon you.
- ☐ Is very demanding and domineering.
- ☐ Is very persistent.
- ☐ Is protective to an *extreme.*
- ☐ Is jealous, possessive, accusatory.

☐ Envies you if things are going well for *you.*

☐ Insensitive to *your* needs.

☐ Needs to *control* everything.

☐ Makes *decisions* for you.

☐ Makes unreasonable, untimely demands to satisfy *his* selfish and immediate desires.

☐ Expects you to *anticipate* his every desire.

☐ Wants you to *drop* what you're doing to please him.

☐ Gives you the silent treatment if you violate one of his *petty* rules.

☐ Is *often* deceptive, deceitful.

☐ Often *promises* great changes.

☐ Usually breaks promises

☐ Has *his* money for *his* enjoyment.

☐ Refuses to contribute financially to the *household* budget.

☐ Prefers to be *blameless* for marriage, family and job failures.

☐ Claims your "verbal abuse" (actual or exaggerated) *justifies* his behavioral response.

☐ Is often sexually forceful, demanding, selfish or abusive.

☐ Demands that you engage in *bizarre* sexual activities.

☐ Sometimes *withholds* sex to punish or manipulate.

☐ Tends to *embarrass* you.

☐ Bad mouth's you in front of who's ever around.

☐ Likes to *humiliate* you in front of his friends.

☐ Directs his *anger* at you.

☐ Frightens you with his *temper.*

☐ Often *increases* level of abuse/violence as cycle continues.

☐ Becomes more and more *dangerous* to live with.

☐ Attempts to *kill* you, himself or both.

BLAME-THROWING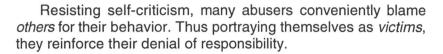

Resisting self-criticism, many abusers conveniently blame *others* for their behavior. Thus portraying themselves as *victims*, they reinforce their denial of responsibility.

Do any of the following traits match your partner's behavior pattern?

◘ Harshly critical.

◘ Manipulative.

◘ Conducts spot checks.

◘ Constantly needs to correct you.

◘ Needs to yell to get his point across.

◘ Monitors your phone calls and appointments.

◘ Interrogates the children as to your habits.

◘ Conducts surveillance of your activities.

◘ Demonstrates a lack of respect for you.

◘ Strenuously resists voluntary treatment programs.

◘ Seeks to negotiate counseling programs which are not court-ordered or undertaken willingly and voluntarily.

TABULATION

Your partner certainly need *not* exhibit *all* of the above character traits or personality disorders to quality as an abuser or potential abuser. Whatever the number, the results need to be analyzed. Your safety and well-being is dependent upon how well you pay attention to the significance of the results.

☞ A *small* number should put you into an *alert* mode.

☞   A *higher* number should indicate a need for genuine *concern.*

☞   A *large* number should signify cause to carefully *re-examine* the relationship and consider *termination.*

DID YOU CHANGE YOUR NAME ?

If you are being referred to as his "old lady" or "the wife", pay close attention. If he has "forgotten" your name, you soon may be *depersonalized* to the point where *you* are who and what *he* wants you to be.

Your new name may become "dumb bitch" or "lazy bitch".... perhaps "fat bitch" or "ugly bitch." You may be known as "slut" or "whore" or worse, a slang word for the female genitals.

Whatever the insulting, degrading and anti-female name may be, you are no longer a person....you are instead an object or something less than fully human.

Since it is not possible to abuse someone you truly love or at least consider your peer or equal, you have now been relegated to the level of sub-human *property.*

SUBSTANCE ABUSE

It is vitally important that you *recognize* substance abuse in your relationship. Though drug or alcohol use is *not* believed to cause spousal abuse, it is often used as an *excuse* for such behavior.

Even if your partner is not physically abusive, his dependency on drugs or alcohol will create a multitude of *problems*, both large and small, within the relationship.

The battering partner who is a substance abuser must take responsibility for *both* problems. Substance treatment alone will *not* stop the battering, just as a spouse abuse counseling program alone will *not* curtail substance abuse. Coexisting problems require *dual* counseling.

PORNOGRAPHY

Many couples enjoy....though not necessarily equal in enthusiasm....using adult films as a means of entertainment and/or stimulation for their love-making.

If your partner *habitually* selects or expresses a *preference* for films depicting women in submissive roles....as victims of *sadistic* acts where the males are totally in charge....beware of the *possible* implications.

On the subject of "love-making"....ask yourself if your partner is truly making *love* to you or is he just having *sex* with you.

STAKING HIS CLAIM

He's beginning to get his hooks into you. You'll know he's about to declare "ownership" when unwarranted and un-reasonable *suspicion* begins to set in.

Any eye contact, however innocent or innocuous, with another man can become the basis for suspicion (i.e., saying good morning to the mailman or smiling politely at the waiter).

Once suspicion surfaces, accusations begin to fly. His best way to "protect you" is to *isolate* you. If you don't happily comply, the fists begin to fly.

KEY POINT

Keep in mind that the more socially ingratiating the *abuser*, the more *difficult* it becomes for the *abused* to be *believed*.

THE VICTIM

Do any of these Personal Behavior traits apply to you?

☐ Gravitated toward second or third *abusive* relationship because it felt "normal."

☐ You value relationships more than *yourself.*

☐ Stifle or block *feelings.*

☐ Have *low* self-esteem.

☐ Feel ashamed, unworthy, sense of self-loathing.

☐ Feel *negative* about your body.

☐ Socially *isolated.*

☐ Feeling *stigmatized.*

☐ Asking: "Why me?"

☐ Withdrawn from family.

☐ Lying about your bruises and injuries.

☐ Unable to assess *danger* accurately.

☐ Losing interest in children's welfare.

☐ Losing touch with *self.*

☐ Losing touch with *reality.*

☐ Suffering from *stress* disorder.

☐ Frightened by *any* kind of noise.

☐ Accident-prone.

☐ Over-indulging in *alcohol.*

☐ Abusing medications.

☐ Resorting to illicit *drugs.*

☐ Have *fear* of taking action.

☐ Have sense of *shame*

☐ Feel helpless.

☐ Have sense of *defeat.*

☐ Feel *trapped.*

☐ Anticipating and preparing for *failure.*

☐ Have fear of losing *sanity.*

☐ Depressed.

☐ Contemplating homicide or suicide.

RELATIONSHIP'S EFFECT UPON THE VICTIM ☑

Due to the abusive behavior of your *partner*, do you recognize *yourself* in this picture?

☐ Economically *dependent.*

☐ Believe in "promises."

☐ Expect change of luck *soon.*

☐ Maintain faith in partner's *impending* "lucky break."

☐ Believe that short-term suffering will bring about "long-term" happiness.

☐ Believe *self* at fault.

☐ Emotionally *dependent.*

☐ Must consult *partner* before making any decisions.

☐ Must always consider how he will *react* to your actions or decisions.

☐ Unable to please partner.

☐ Allow repression and restrictions by partner.

☐ Keep *quiet* rather than upset him.

☐ Accept *all* blame and guilt.

☐ Constantly *apologize* to him.

☐ Frequently apologize to others for *his* behavior.

☐ Make *excuses* for partner.

☐ Is ordered to or feel compelled to *lie* for him.

☐ Feel the need to *explain* why he acts the way he does.

☐ Feel the need to *hide* valuables.

- ☐ Accept life's misery, just as your *mother* did.
- ☐ Feel *compelled* to please him.
- ☐ Continuously give in to avoid *upsetting* him.
- ☐ Accept your *punishment* when you've done "wrong."
- ☐ You know he'll come home *demanding* sex because he's been out drinking.
- ☐ Accept role as "sex slave."
- ☐ Flinch every time he raises his *voice.*
- ☐ Can't fall asleep until *he* does.
- ☐ Afraid of partner.
- ☐ You fear him showing up at your *job.*
- ☐ Expect to be hit or punished in some way if you "screwed up."
- ☐ Cannot express opinions or feelings *freely.*
- ☐ Need "*permission*" from partner for routine undertakings.
- ☐ Strive to do things "*perfectly*" for her partner.
- ☐ Must give a daily *report* to him when he gets home.
- ☐ Is constantly *criticized* despite all-out efforts to please.
- ☐ Is beginning to *believe* all the bad things she's accused of.
- ☐ May still *love* partner.
- ☐ Judgment of lethality potential *deteriorates* over time.
- ☐ Contemplate or attempt *homicide* of partner.

LOCKED AWAY ?

Keep in mind that *isolation* of the *abused* helps prevent *revelation* of the *abuser.*

BATTERED WOMEN'S SYNDROME

This behavioral phenomenon consists of a series of common characteristics which appear in women who are physically and psychologically abused over an *extended* period of time by the dominant male in their lives. These women generally *do not* leave their mates, do not inform friends or police and fear *increased* aggression against themselves.

BWS is often seen in cases where a woman claims *self-defense* upon being charged with killing her husband or boyfriend.

BWS COMPONENTS

1. **Tension-Building Stage,** whereby the woman suffers minor beatings and tries to *placate* her partner.

2. **Acute Battering Incident,** which may be provoked by either an *external* event involving the man *or* by the woman finally getting *angry* at him.

3. **Period of Contribution,** wherein the man will often plead for forgiveness and promise to stop beating his partner.

4. **Resumption of Abuse,** which sooner or later results in the continuation of threatening and violent behavior.

WHEN BATTERED WOMEN KILL

The following risk factors pertain to women who *perceive* that they are *about* to be killed:

1. Frequency of assault

2. Severity of injuries

3. Frequency and severity of sexual assault

4. Frequency of intoxication

5. Extent of drug consumption

6. Threats to kill

7. Suicide attempts/threats by woman

MAN VS. WOMAN

The *male* partner is more apt to:

- Hunt down and kill the female partner who has left him.

- Plan a murder-suicide.

- Kill in response to a revelation or discovery of spousal infidelity.

- Kill following lengthy periods of coercive abuse and assault.

- Commit familicidal massacres.

- Kill in a climate of aggression as opposed to self-defense.

PATTERNS OF ABUSE

To the detriment of far too many victims, the recognition of domestic violence is *limited* to the detection of a pattern of acute violent incidents. Unfortunately, a pattern may not emerge for months, even years in some cases.

As the victim attempts to identify a pattern of abuse, it is most often the acute incident, the most obvious form of abusive behavior, which stands out vividly in the recollection process.

In many cases, a pattern of abuse can be established and identified *before* the subject's behavior completes a full cycle or a repeat of such cycle.

A batterer's behavioral traits can be demonstrated in a wide variety of mannerisms, habits, expressions, reactions, idiosyncracies, etc. Such diversity dilutes a standardized method of applying strict rules of interpretation since each relationship is distinct and unique.

Victims and those who come to their aid, need a *framework* for measuring and analyzing the assorted types of coercive behaviors which encompass domestic violence.

Without such a tool, the abuse may not be identified at the most advantageous time, that being the *early* stages of development. It may not be identified until *several* acute incidents have occurred. In fact, it may not be identified until long after the initial onset of violence.

Any delay in identifying abusive tendencies and behavior is a plus for the *abuser.* Delay buys time and provides opportunities to impose assorted controls and "trapping devices" (i.e., being sole financial officer, dictating procreation policy, imposing repressive conditions resulting in isolation from family and friends, etc.)

Identification of abuse is dependent upon the interpretation of *motives*, lest they be perceived as basic declarations of "life-style" decisions. If your input, suggestions, opinions, thoughts, ideas, desires, etc. are almost always discarded, you know you are being *controlled.*

The batterer's need for power and control are usually evident in *all* phases of domestic violence and can be witnessed in the various types of coercive behavior and the *patterns* in which those behaviors emerge.

DISCOVERING PATTERNS   ◯◯◯◯

- In the *early* stages of the relationship, the intensity and severity of abuse is usually low, thereby concealing a "pattern."

- A relatively minor occurrence of violence may be perceived by the victim and others as an *isolated* incident.

- What appears to be sincere expressions of remorse coupled with persuasive promises never to repeat such behavior very often *coax* the victim to remain and " work things out."

- When considerable *time* passes between acute incidents, it becomes difficult to identify a *clear* pattern of violence.

- These lengthy intervals provide time and opportunity for the batterer to play on his partner's *emotions.*

- The victim's *investment* in the relationship provides stimulus for her to *accept* her partner's encouraging sales pitch during the de-escalation phase.

- As time passes, the effectiveness of the de-escalation phase will wear thin due to *too many* broken promises and *too little* substantial change for the better.

- As de-escalation *loses* its effectiveness, the batterer will resort to *other* means to maintain control.

- For many, the de-escalation phase will begin to disappear altogether, *replaced* by fear, the primary tool for trapping and controlling the victim.

- Violence will usually *increase* in frequency and severity over time.

REALITY CHECK

Somewhere along the way, you must say to yourself, this is *not* love....this is not even a relationship. He couldn't possibly care for me and treat me the way he does. This is insanity and I can't take it any longer.

INTERCHANGEABLE TERMS:

Although the word **"he"** or **"she"** is used throughout, it is nonetheless a generic term for **"he/she"** as applicable.

Words such as **"partner"** are also widely used but are generic for spouse, lover, live-in, boy friend, girl friend, etc. as applicable.

The word **"batter"** is interchangeable with assault, beat and physically abuse.

This page intentionally left blank.

Part 1 - C

PREVENTION

 T here are two aspects to consider when discussing the PREVENTION of domestic violence: the *inception* of abuse from a *suspected* abuser in a **New Relationship** -and- the *pattern* of abuse from a *confirmed* abuser in an **Established Relationship**.

The *first* instance is more difficult to prevent because the victim may be suspicious *but* is often caught off guard when the *first* act of violence occurs. Suspicions should have been generated and *acted upon* from the "recognition" stage. When numerous hazard signals are *not recognized* or are *ignored*, the first installment of abuse is almost assured.

In the *second* instance however, the victim is (or should be) alert, prepared and ready to act when the suspected abuser steps *over the line* and declares by *word or action*, that he intends to *dominate* the relationship through fear, intimidation, threats or force (or any combination thereof) and exercise his "right" to subdue, control and punish his partner.

NEW RELATIONSHIP

Think of a new relationship as a special opportunity....a unique chance to *learn* about someone *before* getting too serious or too involved. Take advantage of your strategic position... remaining in control of the situation....with one hand always on the ejection seat.

GETTING ACQUAINTED

Like cancer, *early detection* of an abusive personality offers the best chances to *avoid* becoming a *victim*. As the relationship intensifies and more and more emotions are invested, the inevitable occurs: *flaws* are found in the "special" person. Very often, the party discovering these flaws will rationalize *(make excuses)* and minimize *(overlook)* their importance or impact on the relationship.

Depending upon the particular people involved, the severity of the flaws and their ability to adjust, the mix may be manageable and relatively harmless. Recognizing that no one is perfect, a couple can maintain enthusiasm in the face of uncertainty with a *sensible* and *mature* outlook.

RESEARCH AND INVESTIGATE

You've met someone at a bar, a nightclub, a grocery check-out line, the library or airport waiting area. He's interested, you're interested. He seems nice, really nice. But remember, he's a *complete* stranger.

If you pursue the matter, there are some tactics you can follow to possibly *prevent* a problem with your "catch," such as:

☐ Request his home and work *phone* numbers. If he's hesitant or unwilling, ask yourself *why*.

☐ Whenever possible....and using the utmost of discretion... seek to meet with the former partner(s). They may show you a side of your "catch" that you didn't know existed -or- confirm annoying suspicions which linger unanswered.

☐ Check the public-access computer at your local courthouse for any *records* of a criminal, civil or domestic nature. Federal Bankruptcy Court records may reveal *problems* of a financial nature.

☐ Check the reverse directory at your public library to look up his address to ascertain who lives there.

☐ Check the Property Assessor's Office to ascertain who owns the property where he claims to live.

☐ Finances permitting and circumstances warranting, engage the services of a private investigator to determine or verify the marital, employment and financial status of the subject as well as any *criminal* history or "*skeletons*" lurking in his closet.

Does all of this seem cold, sneaky and impersonal? Perhaps. But many women have *saved* themselves a mountain of *heartache* by preempting a relationship that surely would have led to abuse and violence.

"GETTING TO KNOW YOU"

As the *message* of the lyrics proclaim, get to know *all* about him. Some added advice: as *much* and as *quickly* as is reasonably possible.

Get down to *specifics* to ascertain any tell-tale *signs* of impending trouble such as:

■ Past relationships; *why* did they dissolve?
■ What does he *expect* in a relationship?
■ What are his pet peeves?
■ Are they reasonable or are they *control-oriented*?

■ How does he handle stress and disappointment?

■ What about anger?

BAD VIBES

If something about the new relationship doesn't "feel right," back off as soon as possible. The *longer* you wait, the *more* time the abuser has to play with your head. The *more* he sees you, the *more* he may consider you "*his.*"

JUDGMENT CALL

If you accept a few negative traits in the beginning and a few more begin to emerge, take it as a final warning before you're "stuck" with him. The *more* time devoted to the relationship, the *stronger* the bond becomes. Your chances to *escape* become significantly *diminished*.

PREMARITAL VIOLENCE

If there is violence in a premarital relationship, you can be almost *assured* that violence will occur *after* the ceremony.

FOR BETTER OR WORSE

You may think, I'll *marry* him and *straighten* him out. Think again! Legalizing the union will not improve his *behavior.* If anything, it will probably alter his habits for the worst.

As a married man, he may feel trapped with someone he doesn't really love....or he may feel *relieved* now that he's got you *exactly* where he wants you.

Thus, you have jumped out of the proverbial frying pan and into the fire.

BENEFIT OF DOUBT ?

As to the "Recognition" warning signs, it *may* be possible that there is a *logical* explanation for *some* negative behavior demonstrated during the initial evaluation period. The rule of thumb however should be: the *more* negatives displayed over a *repeated* number of times, the *more* likely that the person *has* abusive tendencies in his personality which *you* alone will *not* change.

It is when several **"Warning Signs"** are *not addressed* or too many **"Caution Signs"** are *overlooked* or even one **"Danger Sign"** is *ignored* that trouble is on the horizon. At that point, negatives *cannot* be turned into positives; faults *cannot* be turned into virtues. It's usually *too late*.

PREDISPOSITION

Every couple will face problems, difficulties, obstacles, setbacks, etc. to one degree or another. This does *not* predestine a relationship to abusive behavior. However, if one party has a PREDISPOSITION towards violence, these external *pressures* may set the stage for abuse.

VULNERABILITY

If you value a relationship *more* than you value *yourself*, your partner....knowing that you will stay *despite* the abuse....can:

1. Take you for granted.

2. Take advantage of you.

3. Mistreat or abuse you.

SENDING SIGNALS

Do you "announce" to those around you (family, friends, co-workers, etc.) by your *self-diminishing* behavior, demeanor, work habits, expressions, appearance, mannerisms, etc.) that you are "available" for mistreatment? If so, personal *attitudes* must change.

NEAR - FATAL ATTRACTION

You may have asked yourself: "What's wrong with me? I keep falling into dominating relationships!" The reasons may be easy to explain. They involve *normal* human *emotions* centering upon underlying **needs:**

❶   **Love / Affection** - this need can get out of control if you reach out to others at the *expense* of your own *self-esteem.* The results are often fruitless and unrewarding.

❷   **Intimacy** - this need can become *compulsive,* thereby exposing your *vulnerabilities* to others. The results are often frustrating.

❸   **Preserving Relationship** - this need can go *off balance* when you value the *relationship* more than you value *yourself* as a person. The results can be an open invitation to be taken advantage of.

ESTABLISHED RELATIONSHIP

At this point, the relationship is deemed to be "established." Perhaps he's already moved in....perhaps you're carrying his child....perhaps you really love him, or believe that you do. But by now you realize that he's not the gentleman that you thought he was. He's roughed you up more than once. His temper frightens you. It's becoming apparent that he intends to control your life by whatever means he chooses. You seem to have passed the point of no return. You need help.

SELF - HELP

There are things *you* can do to begin to apply the brakes, slow down the process and possibly reverse the effects of abuse in your life:

❏ Stop blaming *yourself* for the abuse and violence in your relationship.

❏ Refuse to take responsibility for your *partner's* abusive behavior.

❏ Realize that before you can take good care of your children, you must take good care of *yourself.*

❏ Recognize that *your* thoughts and feelings are *legitimate* and *deserving* of consideration.

❏ Allow yourself to make *mistakes* and know that you do *not* have to be perfect.

❏ Begin to feel *good* about yourself and your ability to function as an *adult.*

❏ Accept and deal with *reality*, not what was or what might have been.

❏ Accept your *right* to self-direction.

❏ Refuse to allow *anyone* to treat you in an *abusive* manner.

❏ Devote time and effort into having a healthy relationship with yourself.

❏ Defy the major rule in an abusive household - that there is nothing wrong; that no outside help is needed; that any problems should be kept within the family.

❏ Sign up for a self-defense course, free if possible (offered by a public service organization) or commercial, if necessary and affordable.

PREVENTIVE MEASURES

Although you cannot directly control your partner's behavior, you must *plan viable options* on how you will respond to the danger that such behavior presents.

■ DURING/JUST BEFORE VIOLENT INCIDENT:

▣ Determine which of the following offers the safest means of exit: doors, windows, staircases, elevators, fire escape?

▣ Keep extra car keys in a designated location.

▣ Give children, family member, neighbor, etc., pre-arranged signal or code word for notifying the police.

▣ Instruct children on how to call police in the event that you are unable to.

▣ Have a safe destination and an alternate destination in mind.

▣ Whenever possible, do not allow arguments to develop in confined areas (i.e., bathrooms, hallways, stairwells, etc.) or areas where dangerous instruments are located (i.e., kitchen, garage, workshop, etc.).

■ WITHIN THE HOME: (As Finances Permit)

- ▣ Obtain and use an answering machine to *screen* your telephone calls.

- ▣ Change door locks and install "peep holes."

- ▣ Replace wooden entry doors with steel or metal doors.

- ▣ Install window locks and/or bars.

- ▣ Keep windows and doors locked.

- ▣ Install additional locks and/or security system.

- ▣ Install exterior, sensor-type security lights.

- ▣ Keep first aid supplies on hand.

- ▣ Install smoke detectors or check batteries in existing units.

- ▣ Purchase fire extinguisher for each floor.

- ▣ Purchase rope ladder for second floor, emergency escape.

- ▣ Remove exterior objects which can be used to facilitate forced entry.

- ▣ Keep the car locked, tank filled and in the garage if possible.

- ▣ Request that a trusted neighbor call the police if they see your partner on or about the premises.

- ▣ In extreme cases where the risk of danger is severe, explore the feasibility of obtaining a "panic alarm" from a security company. These remote controlled devices allow the user to summon *immediate* police assistance, circumventing the need to call by telephone.

■ AT WORK:

■ Enter and leave the building at irregular times and locations, if possible.

■ Inform your supervisor and security personnel of your situation.

■ Request cooperative effort to help screen your personal calls.

■ IN PUBLIC:

■ Travel in open areas via well lit streets and sidewalks.

■ Shop and conduct your personal business at times and places which differ from when you were residing with your partner.

■ Whenever possible, socialize in a safe setting with persons who have your best interests in mind.

■ PROTECTING YOUR CHILDREN:

■ Orient your children on the concept of *strategic* planning.

■ Instruct person in care of children (school, day care, sitter, etc.) who *may* and who *may not* pick them up.

■ Inform children how to make *collect* calls in the event that they are *abducted.*

■ ORDER OF PROTECTION:

■ Know where it is at all times, preferably on your person.

■ Keep an up-to-date copy in your "Evacuation Pack."

■ Check with your local police agency to ascertain if they have access to your order.

■ Inform *selected* persons of the existence of the order (i.e., trusted friend/relative/neighbor/co-worker; employer, attorney, etc.).

SURVIVAL TIPS

☐ Read between the lines with statements such as "Promise me you'll never leave me no matter what" ....or.... "You're mine now and no one else will ever have you (or love you)." Are these innocuous expressions of true affection or substantial evidence of subtle selfishness?

☐ Exercise intuition and good judgment whenever possible.

☐ If you *know* he's abusive, do not *cohabitate*, lest you become his *hostage*.

☐ Familiarize yourself with family laws, remedial procedures, shelter locations and victim resources *before* you need to use them.

☐ Consider opening a *savings* account for a sense of independence and emergency reserves.

☐ Keep an emergency stash of *cash* in a secure location or with a trusted neighbor.

☐ Keep in mind that use of a telephone credit card will, upon receipt of the next statement, reveal the recent number that you called. To *remedy* this, keep spare change on hand, call collect if possible or ask to use a friend's phone/card in an emergency.

☐ Periodically review and rehearse evacuation *plans* and *alter* as necessary.

☐ Attend workshops and seminars on *victimization.*

☐ Read up on the various self-help *books* on the market (i.e., relationships gone astray, taking charge of your life, rebuilding your confidence, becoming assertive, etc.).

☐ Avoid resorting to the use of narcotics or alcohol. The costs in physical, financial and emotional terms far outweigh any gain derived from a temporary "escape."

☐ Avoid resorting to tranquilizers, pain killers or sleeping pills as well. Substance abuse can significantly reduce your awareness and ability to react to an impending assault.

☐ Avoid personal contact with your partner, if possible. Instead communicate via telephone, mail or third party (excluding your children).

☐ If your partner wants to *enter* the premises to remove his personal belongings, *insist* that he do so in the presence of a law enforcement officer.

EVACUATION PACK

■ DOCUMENTS:
- ❑ Apt. Lease (or House Deed)
- ❑ Birth Certificate(s)
- ❑ Green Card
- ❑ Life Ins. Policy
- ❑ Military/Discharge
- ❑ Passport(s)
- ❑ School Records
- ❑ Social Sec. Card(s)
- ❑ V. A. Benefits
- ❑ Welfare Ident.
- ❑ Work Permit

■ FINANCIAL:
- ❑ Bank Books(s)
- ❑ Cash/ATM Card
- ❑ Checkbook
- ❑ Credit/Debit Cards
- ❑ Food Stamps
- ❑ Invest. Records
- ❑ Loan Pymt. Books
- ❑ Mortgage Coupons

■ MARITAL:
- ❑ Case/File Nos.
- ❑ Divorce Agreement
- ❑ Protection Order, Copy
- ❑ Separation Agreement

■ MEDICAL:
- ❑ Health Ins. Card
- ❑ Medical Records(s)
- ❑ Medications
- ❑ Vaccination Record(s)

■ MISCELLANEOUS:
- ❑ Address/Tel. Book
- ❑ Child's Favorite Toy
- ❑ Clothing, Extra
- ❑ Jewelry
- ❑ Keys (House, Job)
- ❑ Membership I.D.s
- ❑ Notes/Records
- ❑ Personal Items
- ❑ Photos
- ❑ Safe Dep. Box Info.

■ PHONE NUMBERS:
- ❑ Abuse Counselor
- ❑ Attorney
- ❑ Family Court
- ❑ Help Hotline
- ❑ Job Supervisor
- ❑ Police Department
- ❑ Spiritual Advisor
- ❑ Taxi Service
- ❑ Victim's Advocate
- ❑ Women's Shelter

■ VEHICLE:
- ❑ Driver's License
- ❑ Insurance Card
- ❑ Keys (Door-Trunk-Ign.)
- ❑ Registration

NOTE: as the relationship deteriorates, you should begin to gather and stash away, *duplicate* copies of *important* records, documents, licenses and certificates since your partner may try to hide or destroy these documents in order to delay or prevent your departure.

Categories of concern should include legal, financial, medical, marital and personal affairs. Also keep a duplicate record of vital account, file, case, and reference *numbers.*

Utilize the "Evacuation Pack" and other such checklists found in Part 6-B as a *guide.*

SALVAGEABLE RELATIONSHIPS

If it is determined by both parties, preferably in conjunction with a skilled counselor, that an established relationship can be saved, the following specific areas should be addressed:

✓ Communication techniques.

✓ Handling disagreements.

✓ Handling resentment.

✓ Demonstrating care and affection.

✓ Maintaining one's own identity within the relationship.

✓ Being dependable and consistent.

✓ Budgeting and handling finances.

✓ Dealing with children and/or step-children.

✓ Respecting one another.

✓ Demonstrating trust and support.

✓ Accepting responsibility for self.

✓ Sharing parental duties and responsibilities.

✓ Setting positive example within home.

✓ Sharing responsibility fairly.

✓ Practicing teamwork running household.

✓ Making equitable decisions.

✓ Practicing negotiation to resolve disagreements.

✓ Learning how to compromise.

✓ Accepting change.

DOMESTIC VIOLENCE PREVENTION PROGRAM

The primary goals of a basic prevention program are to:

① Reduce the *number* of incidents of family violence.

② Render *assistance* through appropriate referrals and counseling.

③ Identify and *arrest* offenders.

WHAT HELPS ?

✓ Seeking assistance helps.

✓ Calling the police helps.

✓ Arresting the offender helps.

✓ Prosecuting the offender helps.

✓ Supporting the victim helps.

✓ Counseling the victim helps.

✓ Punishing the offender helps.

✓ Counseling the offender helps.

Chapter Two

ABUSE BEGINS

❏ Part 2 - A   VICTIMIZATION

❏ Part 2 - B   LEGISLATION

❏ Part 2 - C   ORIGINATION

This page intentionally left blank.

Part 2 - A

VICTIMIZATION

We know that victims come in both genders and all ages, regardless of race, color, creed, sexual orientation, health, occupation, education, professional background or marital or social status.

Victimization can occur between dating partners or an engaged couple; a present or former spouse or live-in; a parent and a biological, adopted, foster, step or unborn child; or an elderly family member residing in the home.

In this segment, we will examine the "victim" of domestic violence more closely.

PRESENT AND FUTURE VICTIMS

The key component of abuse or violence is a *relationship* between two people who are drawn together....whether as friends, lovers, spouses, parents or family....which goes *off balance*....out of a compelling need or desire by one party to *control* the other.

MARITAL RAPE

Rarely *discussed* with others out of shame and embarrassment and rarely *reported* to the police out of a sense of secrecy and futility, the "wifely duty" can become a *criminal* act when it is accompanied by:

☉ Threats of assault for non-compliance.

☉ The use of injurious physical force.

- Abusive tactics used to coerce the victim to engage in undesirable acts.

- Acts of sexual mutilation.

DATE RAPE

"Date rape" is pre-marital sexual abuse or violence occurring between persons who are acquaintances or in a dating situation. Victims can be adults *or* adolescents.

As a victim or parent, one must be vigilant to *prevent* date rape from turning into *marital* rape.

As a further preventive measure, the dangers of abusive *friendships* and dating *relationships* should be included in *school* curricula.

STALKING

Are you a stalking victim? A stalker is a person, usually a male, who demonstrates an *abnormal* fixation with another person. For purposes of our discussion, we will not address the "celebrity stalker" though we should thank him for prompting passage of anti-stalking laws in many states in the early 90's.

The "relationship stalker" is *known* to the victim, usually through an intimate relationship or work. When the relationship ends, this stalker seeks to *avenge* his rejection. Such interpersonal relationship cases have a high *potential* to end in a tragic incident.

Some stalkers are *obsessed* with their prey; vowing never to stop, never to allow their former mate to date another *peacefully* again. Obsessive-compulsive stalking is often accompanied with a barrage of unwanted phone calls, cards, letters, flowers and gifts.

The "relationship stalker" commits a high percentage of violent acts. The more personal *contacts* the stalker makes, the more *dangerous* he becomes. Stalking, accompanied by threats of violence, *must* be taken *very* seriously.

PRANK PHONE CALLS

One of life's more exasperating nuisances, they can run the gamut from being mildly annoying to downright frightening.

Sooner or later, almost everyone....regardless of their domestic situation....will be victimized by the prank caller, whose intentions may range from simply wanting to *bother* someone as a joke, to wanting to sexually or physically *harm* their victims.

What can you do to *minimize* the prank caller's use of *your* phone?

☎ Remember that it's *your* phone and you must learn to take better *control* of it.

☎ The *instant* you realize that a call is not *legitimate* (i.e., silence, heavy breathing, profanity, disguised voices, unacceptable comments, etc.) You *must* hang up!

☎ Keep *repeating* the hang up procedure as necessary.

☎ *Never* display or express your annoyance, fear or curiosity. This only *rewards* the caller and provides added *incentive* for him to continue.

☎ If finances permit, utilize caller-identification and/or call-blocking features, available through your telephone company.

☎ Use your answering machine to *screen* your calls. Answer *only* those calls which you care to or need to.

☎ Save answering machine tapes containing *evidence* of unlawful communications.

☎ Report cases of harassing or threatening calls to your phone company and local police.

☎ If necessary, consider *changing* your number to an *unlisted* one and then use the utmost care in giving out your new listing.

OUTSIDE INTERFERENCE

Many victims of domestic violence may be further abused and put upon by the family and friends of their abusers, who either believe the lies and distortions about them, have similar pro-abuse attitudes or are just blindly loyal to an extreme.

This added and equally unwanted abuse *usually* takes the form of verbal assault and petty forms of harassment. If they cannot be ignored, in the hopes that they will soon subside, police intervention may be necessary to deter further problems and to prevent escalation to more serious acts of criminal behavior.

As a victim, you may want to make an effort to explain or defend your position in the relationship to your detractors. If after the initial attempt you are un-successful, further attempts to tell your side of the story might prove counter-productive. Whatever the case, *resist* the urge to retaliate in kind or go on the offensive with these people.

Your *primary* adversary is your partner, whose personal habits and predilections are the *main* source of your domestic distress. Your principal *goal* is to extricate yourself from his clutches and his controlling and abusive lifestyle.

THE FAMILY AS VICTIM

Domestic violence is a *corrosion* of the most *fundamental* unit of American life: the family. A permissive or casual attitude toward domestic violence by any member of society or any segment of the "system" helps to undermine the integrity and stability of the family unit.

Just as motorists, pedestrians and store keepers deserve protection on the street, so do family members deserve protection in the home. A closed door or a drawn curtain should not prevent the enforcement of duly enacted and lawfully applied statutes.

Consequently, public policies which support the family are critical for the survival and nourishment of society. For families to thrive, the destructive forces of domestic violence must be examined, addressed, reduced and ultimately eliminated.

COMMON THREAD

Q. Of the various victims of domestic violence, what characteristics are *most* common to *each* group?

A. Vulnerability, proximity, helplessness, innocence and ignorance (not to be confused with stupidity, ignorance is the *absence* of knowledge).

MOST VULNERABLE

Although the elderly are at a distinct disadvantage, *children*, especially the pre-teen group, are more vulnerable and helpless because of their inability to function on their own in an adult world.

MOST IMPRESSIONABLE

Children are *children*, not miniature adults. Their under-developed minds cannot readily sort out the complexities of the "Good Daddy" one day and the "Bad Daddy" the next. What they *do* see and hear can create a negative, confusing and frightening impression on their *tender*, young minds.

Sadly, criminal behavior demonstrated and tolerated *within* the home becomes an open invitation to violate the law *outside* the home. Abuse *learned* in the home is often *practiced* in the streets, the schoolyards and the classrooms. As time marches on, constant violence becomes the "norm."

Because of the many negative factors that involve children and because of their sheer vastness in numbers, this section will zero in almost entirely on the victimization of children.

CHILD ABUSE

Battered women are more likely to physically abuse their children than non-battered women. If *you* are abusing your children....taking your frustrations out on them or showing them who's boss in a violent manner, *you* need help. If your partner is guilty of such behavior, then *he* needs help. If you are *both* guilty of this practice, your child is in *serious* danger!

THE CHILDREN ARE WATCHING

Some men want an audience when they assert their "right" to control their partner. Unfortunately, and with detrimental side effects, that audience is usually the children.

Boys consequently tend to become aggressive and combative. Girls tend to become passive and withdrawn. Very often, these boys become men who batter their women. The girls tend to become women who accept subservient roles as adult mates.

Not surprisingly, children who *both* witness abuse directed toward a parent *and* experience child abuse themselves, are subject to the most *profound* adverse effects.

CHILDREN AT RISK

The child of a batterer is often "in the way" or is a convenient target for the uncontrolled wrath of the abusive parent. Generally, the more severe the abuse of the mother, the more severe the abuse is to the child. Intervening to defend or protect the mother, further jeopardizes the child's safety.

Male abusers are more likely to victimize a female child than a male child and are more likely to cause severe injuries and fatalities than female abusers.

Female children, residing in violent homes, are more likely to be sexually abused than if residing in non-violent homes.

EFFECTS UPON CHILDREN

The impact of *seeing* and *hearing* episodes of domestic violence is in itself a *form* of child abuse. A *constant* diet of violence or abuse in the home can desensitize a child to its effects, often causing a *continuation* of the problem straight into adulthood.

Child victims are more likely to experience isolation, loneliness, low self-esteem, fear, anxiety, sleeping difficulties, nightmares, and a sense of helplessness. Children exposed to abuse are often insecure and more prone to depression. Prolonged exposure can result in poor health, post-traumatic stress disorder and developmental retardation.

Increased aggression in children, often leads to inadequate impulse control and anti-social behavioral traits, thus resulting in acts of juvenile delinquency.

IT CAN GET WORSE

Such children may:

- Abuse drugs and/or alcohol
- Fail in school and drop out
- Run away from home
- Engage in teen prostitution
- Abuse their friends or dating partners
- Commit sexual offenses
- Engage in criminal acts
- Attempt suicide

UPON REACHING ADULTHOOD

Uncorrected behavior may follow the child along the road to adulthood, poisoning the next generation and retarding their chances of becoming good parents themselves. Such *future* adults may:

- Adopt sociopathic behavior patterns.
- Be unable to form strong, positive and loving bonds of kinship.
- As men, emulate the pattern of domestic violence learned in childhood.
- As women, accept the "inevitability" of victimization as "normal."

AID AND COMFORT

The criminal justice system, medical profession and child abuse prevention agencies must combine resources and energies to *identify* children at risk and implement strategies to protect and heal the innocent victims of domestic violence, *especially* those who are most powerless, the *children* from abusive and violent homes.

Counseling is vitally important with an *immediate* goal to help cushion the painful experience of growing up and attempting to function in an abusive environment and a *long-range* goal of preventing future abusers and future victims.

POSITIVE VALUE

Odd as it may seem, child abuse inflicted by the offending partner can have a *positive* value; it *may* generate the *impetus*, necessary for seeking the *help*, required in dealing with the abusive partner.

SPECIAL CASES

A "victim" is not a stereotypical individual formed from the same mold. There are a variety of special cases or classes of victims who, because of their particular circumstances, have needs which require special consideration and handling.

PREGNANT WOMEN

There are at least *two* victims involved when domestic violence is committed upon a pregnant female. Such cowardly behavior increases the risk of miscarriage, birth defects and low birth-weight babies. A punch or kick to the stomach tells you that the assault is intended for *both* mother and child.

WOMEN OF COLOR

Some women of color, believing that the "system" is tainted with racial and cultural bigotry, may hesitate to initiate outside intervention out of fear that their partners will be dealt with more severely, and that their contemporaries in the community will look upon their actions unfavorably.

While there *may* be a basis for this belief, the reluctance *must* be overcome. Working through an advocacy or support group can help to muster the necessary initiative to pursue the investigation.

On the political-activist front, women of color must be *welcomed* into the fold of those Anglo feminists who, for one reason or another, *may* not be convinced of the urgency to include in their agenda, the unique perspective of these victims.

RURAL WOMEN

Women in rural settings are subject to added *isolation.* The geographical distance between neighboring homes, the virtual absence of public transportation, the sparsity of community services and the inherent lack of anonymity in a small town environment often inhibits the victim from bringing attention to her plight.

"MAIL-ORDER BRIDES"

Modern technology now brings us the mail-order bride via *computer* selection on the global Internet, where women are displayed like trading cards on Web sites, along with some personal, biographical data.

Is it a dream of American life come true, or a would-be world of slavery and abuse for the woman? Is it a safe and harmless way for a man to meet the "ideal" mate, or just a legal means to peddle women into bondage?

Like ordering merchandise through a supply catalog, this method of match-making is as controversial as it is potentially exploitative. Critics charge that the system is decidedly lopsided in favor of the man. Foreign to her husband, his culture and possibly his language, the wife's immigrant status and economic dependence puts the woman at a distinct disadvantage. Those who fail to live up to expectations are in *jeopardy* of being abused in any variety of ways. Options for recourse are *limited*.

Women affected might check with the I.N.S., their native-born country's embassy or a cultural organization sponsored by their fellow citizens.

Men should be *wary* of this process because of the potential for fraud and misrepresentation. Also, the time factor, the cost involved and the bureaucracy of both countries should be cause for serious reconsideration.

IMMIGRANTS

Culture and language may impede the communication process but should never be *barriers* to justice. Interpreters of languages commonly spoken in the community should be available to assist in the intervention and intake process.

PROSTITUTES

Some financially desperate victims of domestic violence resort to selling their bodies in a last-ditch effort to support themselves and their children.

Specialized counseling should be available for those persons who are thus subjugated to a life of prostitution and/or pornography.

LESBIANS AND GAYS

In addition to the violence itself, homosexuals face added difficulties because of their affectional orientation, such as fewer resources, homophobia from the service providers and denial within the homosexual community.

Gay and lesbian victims must work through activist organizations to bring about needed change for their constituents.

DISABLED VICTIMS

Victims with physical disabilities face added difficulty in that few shelters are staffed and equipped to accommodate their special needs. This deficiency in the intervention phase must be addressed by the appropriate agencies.

MALE VICTIMS

Statistically, male victims are in the minority but they must *not* be overlooked. The natural assumption is that a man can take care of himself but that is not true in *all* cases.

Male victims must work to overcome the stigma attached to reporting their being victimized by "the weaker sex." Also, the intervention apparatus must be willing and able to accommodate the male victim of violence within his home.

SELF - DEFENSE

At some point in your relationship you may need to *defend* yourself, your premises or your property. Depending upon the *circumstances*, you may need to employ physical force *or* deadly physical force against your adversary. If any force *is* used, you will want your action to be "justified" under the law.

Since the laws will vary from state to state, we offer herein *suggestions* on questions to ask your local police or your legal counsel....questions pertaining to offensive and defensive behavior as it pertains to your particular domestic situation in your particular state of residency.

Needless to say, using any degree of force against another person, especially deadly force, is *serious* business, with possible civil and criminal *consequences* ....in addition to ethical and moral *ramifications* which could haunt you for a lifetime.

The haphazard or careless use of force against a person who is perceived to be or is in fact a threat to your safety or the safety of another person present will have detrimental effects on all those involved.

Laws and guidelines should ideally be reviewed in *advance* whenever possible to fully understand the legal repercussions of unjustified or irrational behavior against another person.

The essence of your inquiry should be: What constitutes the necessary, authorized, lawful and justifiable use of physical and deadly force against another person?

Assuming a cloak of *immunity* due to a *misunderstanding* of the law can lead to premeditated actions or a spontaneous response, not in keeping with the spirit of the law. Care and discretion in abiding with the law is not merely recommended but is *required* in a civilized society.

DEFENSE OF PERSON

May I use physical force against another to protect myself or a third person against the use or imminent use of physical force?

☐ Suppose I *provoked* or *hit* him first?

May I use *deadly* physical force to defend myself or another against the unlawful use or imminent use of deadly force against me?

☐ Suppose I can retreat to complete *safety* before-hand?

May I use *deadly* physical force to defend myself or another against the commission or attempted commission of a *felony?*

☐ If so, *which* felony/felonies?

DEFENSE OF PREMISES

May I use physical force to prevent or terminate *damage* to my premises?

☐ What about an *attempted* commission of such act?

May I use physical force to prevent or defend my premises against the commission or attempted commission of an act of *trespass?*

☐ Must I be the landlord or tenant of such premises?

May I use *deadly* physical force to prevent or terminate the commission or attempted commission of an act of *arson?*

☐ Must I be the landlord or tenant of such premises?

May I use *deadly* physical force to prevent or terminate the commission or attempted commission of a *burglary?*

☐ Must the building be *occupied* or designated as a *dwelling?*

DEFENSE OF PROPERTY

■ May I use physical force to prevent or terminate the commission or attempted commission of a larceny or *theft* of my property?

☐ What about an act of criminal *mischief* to such property?

ARREST / ESCAPE SITUATIONS

■ May I use physical force to effect an arrest?

☐ Suppose such person is *escaping* from custody?

■ May I use *deadly* physical force to defend myself against the use or imminent use of *deadly* physical force in effecting an arrest or preventing an escape?

☐ May I also act to defend a third person in such situation?

■ May I use *deadly* physical force in effecting an arrest of a person who is in immediate *flight* from a felony?

☐ Which felony/felonies?

■ May I use physical force to assist a Police Officer in *making* an arrest or in *preventing* an escape from custody if so directed by such officer?

☐ What if the arrest is not or was not *authorized* by law?

DISCIPLINE / MISCELLANEOUS

■ As a parent, may I use physical force to maintain discipline?

☐ May a *guardian* use such discipline also?

■ May I use physical force to prevent another person from inflicting *serious* physical injury upon himself?

☐ What if the intended injury is less than serious in nature?

Part 2 - B

LEGISLATION

This segment of the survival guide shall deal with the *law*, albeit in a general way. The **first** portion provides a *checklist* of legal issues of a procedural or remedial nature... issues which cover common areas of contention between domestic partners in turmoil.

As various problems and situations begin to develop and the relationship or family unit begins to deteriorate, questions concerning family law will often arise.

Pertinent procedures and avenues of legal recourse can initially be researched by the lay person and thereafter be clarified by professional legal counsel as may be necessary.

The **second** portion of "Legislation" provides another *check-list*... this one to stimulate the thought process on the possible *criminal* nature of your partner's behavior.

The **third** and concluding portion offers suggested material for *future* legislation....some or all of which you may wish to support... to aid victims and combat the violence which they are subjected to.

ATTENTION REQUIRED

Use this section as a "tickler file." Check issues which may apply to your situation. Research them in a public or law library and/or bring them to the attention of your legal advisor.

■ CHILDREN / DEPENDENTS

❑ Abandonment _____

❑ Abuse / Maltreatment _____

❑ Custody _____

❑ Day Care Program _____

❑ Delinquency _____

❑ Dependency _____

❑ Disabled / Medically Needy _____

❑ Foster Care _____

❑ Guardianship _____

❑ Health / Welfare Services _____

❑ Protective Proceeding _____

❑ Removal by Authorities _____

❑ Restitution _____

❑ Retarded Services _____

❑ Runaway _____

❑ Visitation _____

■ CHILD SUPPORT

❑ Agency Assistance _____

❑ Arrears _____

❑ Blood / DNA Testing _____

❑ Collection Procedures _____

❑ Disability _____

❑ Income Deduction Order _____

❏ Non-Payment _____

❏ Paternity, Establishing _____

❏ Support Order, Permanent _____

❏ Support Order, Temporary _____

❏ Unemployment _____

■ FAMILY / FAMILY COURT

❏ Appeals Process _____

❏ Application Process _____

❏ Contempt of Court _____

❏ Family Offenses _____

❏ Indigent Person _____

❏ Legal Counsel _____

❏ Motion / Petition, Filing for _____

❏ Protection Order, Filing for _____

❏ Services Available _____

■ MARITAL ISSUES

❏ Alimony, Filing for _____

❏ Annulment, Filing for _____

❏ Conciliation Proceeding _____

❏ Divorce / Dissolution _____

❏ Judgment, Motion to Modify _____

❏ Life Insurance _____

❏ Maintenance _____

❏ Property, Distribution of _____

❏ Property, Title / Possession of _____

❏ Separation, Filing for_____

❏ Support Order_____

❏ Void / Voidable Marriage_____

VIOLATIONS OF LAW

At this point, you have failed to **recognize** domestic abuse when it poked its head in your window and you have failed to **prevent** it once it came through the door. Now, your partner is beginning to flex his muscles. So far it's all vocal; but sooner or later he's going to break the law.

This segment breaks down a variety of DOMESTIC-RELATED behavior....either disruptive, intrusive, violent or abusive.... affecting your health, safety, home, property finances and children.

For purposes of *discussion* and *example*, we have compiled this list based on *New York State* law and present it in seven distinct categories. Although the specific wording of the various statutes among the various states will differ, the *essence* of the act is such that you can use this compilation as a *checklist* to gain a clearer picture of where your partner stands in relation to any criminal behavior occurring within *your* relationship.

Review the synopsis which accompanies each offense. It states that portion or portions of the offense which deals primarily or significantly with *domestic* and/or *family* situations.

If your partner has committed any of the acts listed and described herein, chances are he has violated the law in *your* state.

How many check marks will you come up with for **your** partner?

Group 1: PRE-CONTACT; NON-PHYSICAL

❏ **Adultery** **Misdemeanor**
engages in sexual intercourse when *he* or the *other* person has a living *spouse*.

❏ **Attempt to Commit a Crime** **Misd. - Felony**
intentionally engages in conduct which *tends* to effect commission of a particular crime.

❏ **Bigamy** **Felony**
contracts/purports to contract a marriage when *he* or the *other* person has a living *spouse.*

❏ **Burglary 2°** **Felony**
knowingly enters/remains unlawfully in *a building* with intent to commit a *crime* therein.

❏ **Coercion 2°** **Misdemeanor**
compels/induces one to do: that which one has a right to *abstain from* -or- abstain from that which one has a *right to do* by instilling *fear* that someone will cause *harm* re: health, safety, career, finances, etc.

❏ **Communication Info., Obtain** **Misdemeanor**
knowing he is *unauthorized*, attempts/obtains info. re: *record* of telephone/telegraph communication from utility company by deception/stealth/etc.

❏ **Communication, Tamper With**   **Misdemeanor**
knowingly and without consent of sender/receiver, opens/
reads/divulges contents of *sealed* communication -or-
attempts/obtains info. re: contents of *telephone/telegraph*
communication from utility company in any manner.

❏ **Disorderly Conduct**   **Violation**
engages in a variety of acts/behavior intending to or recklessly
creating *risk* of causing inconvenience, annoyance or alarm
ordinarily, but not necessarily in public.

❏ **Drugs/Narcotics in Public**   **Violation**
appears in public place under *influence* of drugs/narcotics and
may *endanger* self/others/property or *annoy* those in vicinity.

❏ **Eavesdropping**   **Felony**
unlawfully engages in wiretapping/mechanical overhearing of
a *conversation* -or- intercepting/accessing of an electronic
communication.

❏ **Harassment 2°**   **Violation**
with intent to harass/annoy/alarm, *follows* person in or about
public place(s) -or- commits acts which serve no legitimate
purpose and alarm or seriously annoy another.

❏ **Harassment, Aggravated 2°**   **Misdemeanor**
with intent to harass/annoy/threaten/alarm, *communicates*
anonymously or otherwise (or causes same) by phone/
telegram/mail/written communication -or- *calls* with or w/o
conversation, with no valid purpose.

❏ **Marriage License, Unlawfully Procure**   **Misdemeanor**
procures license when *he* or the *other* person has a living
spouse.

❏ **Trespass**   **Violation**
knowingly enters/remains unlawfully in or upon premises
("building" or real property).

❏ **Trespass, Criminal 2° & 3°**   **Misdemeanor**
knowingly enters/remains unlawfully in a *dwelling* -or- in a
building or upon *real property* which is fenced or enclosed.

Group 2: PHYSICAL CONTACT; PHYSICAL INJURY/FEAR OF

❑ **Assault, Simple**   **Misdemeanor**
intentionally causes physical injury to victim or 3rd person -or-
recklessly causes physical injury to another -or- with *criminal
negligence*, causes physical injury to another via deadly
weapon or dangerous instrument.

❑ **Coercion 1°**   **Felony**
commits 2° by instilling *fear* of physical injury or damage to
property or by compelling/inducing victim to commit/attempt
a *felony* or cause/attempt physical injury to another.

❑ **Contempt, Criminal 1°**   **Felony**
in violation of *Order of Protection*: intentionally/recklessly
causes physical/serious injury.

❑ **Harassment 1° & 2°**   **Viol. - Misd.**
intentionally and repeatedly *harasses* by following in or about
public place(s) or acts so as to cause reasonable *fear* of
physical injury -or- follow with *intent to harass*, annoy or
alarm; or acts so as to alarm or seriously annoy; or subjects/
attempts/threatens physical contact.

❑ **Harassment, Aggravated 2°**   **Misdemeanor**
with intent to harass, annoy, threaten or alarm, subjects/
attempts/threatens *physical contact* due to race, color,
religion or national origin.

❑ **Imprisonment, Unlawful 2°**   **Misdemeanor**
restrains (intentionally and unlawfully restricts movements of)
another person, thereby substantially interfering with their
liberty by force, intimidation or deception.

❑ **Kidnapping 2°**   **Felony**
abducts victim by restraining with intent to *prevent liberation*
by secreting/holding where not likely to be found.

❑ **Larceny, Grand 2° & 4°**   **Felony**
steals property by *extortion:* compels/induces victim to deliver
property to self/3rd person by instilling *fear* of physical injury,

property damage, engaging in or accusing of a crime, institute criminal charges or generally performs any act calculated to harm re: health, safety, business, calling, career, financial condition, reputation or personal relationships.

❏ **Robbery 2° & 3°** **Felony**
forcibly steals property; uses/threatens immediate use of physical force; may cause such injury or display a firearm.

❏ **Victim/Witness, Intimidate 2° & 3°** **Felony**
causes/threatens physical injury to *prevent* communication of criminal information to authorities or causes such injury in *retaliation* for so communicating or recklessly causes such injury while intentionally damaging property in such *retaliation*.

Group 3: PHY. CONTACT; SER. INJURY/DEATH/RISK OF

❏ **Arson 1° & 2°** **Felony**
intentionally and knowingly damages *occupied* building/motor vehicle by fire/explosion.

❏ **Assault, Felonious** **Felony**
intentionally causes to victim/3rd person: serious physical injury, disfigurement, amputation, disability; physical injury via deadly weapon/dangerous instrument -or- *recklessly* causes serious physical injury: via such weapon/instrument or by depraved conduct -or- causes physical impairment via drug.

❏ **Assault, Vehicular** **Felony**
causes serious physical injury through *criminal negligence* while intoxicated or with ability impaired by drugs.

❏ **Burglary 1°** **Felony**
knowingly enters or remains unlawfully in a dwelling with *intent* to commit a *crime* therein and in effecting/therein/ fleeing: is armed with explosive or deadly weapon, uses/ threatens immediate use of dangerous instrument, displays firearm or causes physical injury.

❏ **Contempt, Criminal 1°** **Felony**
intentionally or recklessly causes physical/serious injury in violation of *Order of Protection.*

❑ **Endangerment, Reckless   Misd. - Felony**
recklessly engages in conduct: creating substantial *risk* of serious physical injury -or- grave *risk* of death by depraved indifference to life.

❑ **Homicide, Criminal Negligence   Felony**
causes death of another through criminal negligence.

❑ **Imprisonment, Unlawful 1°   Felony**
intentionally and unlawfully restricts victim's movements in such manner as to expose to *risk* of serious physical injury.

❑ **Kidnapping 1° & 2°   Felony**
abducts victim and restrains: more then 12 hours to inflict physical injury, abuse sexually, advance commission of a felony or terrorize victim or 3rd person -or- prevents liberation by threatening/using deadly physical force.

❑ **Manslaughter   Felony**
recklessly causes death of another -or- with intent to cause serious physical injury, causes death of victim or 3rd person -or- with intent to cause death, causes same to victim or 3rd person under influence of extreme emotional disturbance.

❑ **Manslaughter, Vehicular   Felony**
causes death of another by criminal negligence and is intoxicated or driving while impaired by drugs.

❑ **Menacing   Misd. - Felony**
by physical menace, intentionally attempts/places victim in *fear* of death, imminent serious physical injury or physical injury (display of weapon, firearm, etc. or violation of stay-away provision of duly served Order of Protection upgrades degree) -or- repeatedly follows or acts so as to place victim in reasonable fear of physical/serious injury or death.

❑ **Mischief, Criminal 1°   Felony**
intentionally and unlawfully damages property of another by means of an *explosive*.

❏ **Murder**   **Felony**
  intentionally causes death of victim or 3rd person -or-
  recklessly and with depraved indifference, creates grave risk
  and causes death.

❏ **Robbery 1°**   **Felony**
  forcibly steals property and during/fleeing: causes serious
  physical injury, is armed with deadly weapon, uses/threatens
  immediate use of dangerous instrument or displays firearm.

❏ **Trespass, Criminal 1°**   **Felony**
  knowingly enters or remains unlawfully in a building and
  possesses: explosive, deadly weapon, firearm, rifle or shot-
  gun (with access to ammunition).

❏ **Victim/Witness, Intimidate 1°**   **Felony**
  intentionally causes serious physical injury to another for
  purpose of obstructing/preventing/ etc., the *communication*
  by victim or another of criminal information to *authorities* (or
  in *retaliation* therefor) -or- to *compel* person to swear *falsely.*

❏ **Weapons, Criminal Possession**   **Misd. - Felony**
  possess firearm, specified dangerous articles and deadly instruments, explosives, silencer (type, quantity, intent, previous
  conviction, loaded/unloaded affect severity of offense).

Group 4: SEXUAL OFFENSES

❏ **Abuse, Sexual**   **Misd. - Felony**
  while not married to victim, *touches* clothed/unclothed sexual
  or intimidate parts *without consent* (use of force, victim's age
  or mental incapacity to consent *elevates* degree of offense).

❏ **Abuse, Aggravated Sexual**   **Felony**
  causes physical injury by inserting finger/foreign object in
  vagina, urethra, penis or rectum by force, or upon victim who
  is physically helpless, incapable of consent or under age 11.

❏ **Incest** **Felony**
knowingly marries/engages in sexual/deviate intercourse with person *related* (legitimately/out of wedlock) as an ancestor, descendant, brother or sister (of whole/half blood) uncle, aunt, nephew or niece.

❏ **Misconduct, Sexual** **Misdemeanor**
without consent: male engages in sexual intercourse with female; or a person engages in deviate sexual intercourse with another -or- person engages in sexual conduct with animal or dead human body.

❏ **Rape** **Felony**
engages in sexual intercourse with person to whom not married and is *incapable* of consent -or- a *male* engages in sexual intercourse by *force* or victim is physically helpless and therefore *incapable* of consent. (victim's age can elevate degree of offense).

❏ **Sodomy** **Felony**
engages in deviate sexual intercourse with person: incapable of consent, physically helpless or by force. (victim's age can elevate degree of offense).

Group 5: OFFENSES AGAINST CHILDREN

❏ **Abandonment** **Felony**
being parent/guardian/person legally charged with care/ custody of child under 14, *deserts* such child in any place with *intent* to wholly abandon.

❏ **Assault, Felonious** **Felony**
being 18 or older, with *intent* to cause *physical* injury to child *under* 11, *recklessly* causes *serious physical injury.*

❏ **Assault, Aggravated** **Felony**
being 18 or older, commits felonious assault upon child *under* 11, having *previous conviction* of same within preceding *3 years.*

❏ **Custodial Interference**   **Misd. - Felony**
knowing he has *no legal right* to do so and being *relative* of
child *under* 16, intending to hold permanently or for protracted
period, takes/entices child from lawful custodian. (removal
from state or exposure to health/safety risk elevates degree of
offense)

❏ **Deal With Child Unlawfully 1°**   **Misdemeanor**
knowingly permits child *under* 18 to enter/remain in or upon
place/premises/establishment where *sexual/drug/marihuana*
activity is maintained/conducted -or- gives *alcoholic* beverage
to person *under* 21.

❏ **Falsely Reporting Incident 2°**   **Misdemeanor**
reports to Statewide Central Registry by word or action,
an alleged occurrence/condition of *child abuse/maltreatment*
which did not in fact occur/exist.

❏ **Manslaughter 1°**   **Felony**
being 18 or older, with *intent* to cause physical injury to person
under 11, *recklessly* engages in conduct creating *grave risk* of
serious physical injury, thereby causing *death* of such person.

❏ **Murder 2°**   **Felony**
being 18 or older, with *depraved* indifference to life, *recklessly*
creates *grave risk* of serious physical injury/death to person
under 11, thereby causing death.

❏ **Non-Support**   **Misdemeanor**
being parent/guardian/person legally charged with care/
custody of child *under* 16, unlawfully fails or refuses to *provide*
support when able to do so -or- *becomes* unable by voluntarily
terminating employment, reducing earning capacity or failing
to seek employment.

❏ **Sexual Performance, Child in**   **Felony**
being parent/guardian/custodian of child *under* 16, knowingly
consents to participation in sexual performance.

❏ **Solicitation, Criminal 1°, 3°, 4°** **Misd. - Felony**
being 18 or older, intending that a child *under* 16 engage in
conduct constituting a crime, solicits, requests, etc....or otherwise attempts to cause such child to engage in such conduct
(type of offense *solicited* elevates degree of offense charged).

❏ **Substitution** **Felony**
having been temporarily entrusted with child *under* 1,
substitutes, produces or returns another child with the intent
to deceive.

❏ **Welfare, Endanger** **Misdemeanor**
being parent/guardian/person legally charged with care/
custody of child *under* 18, fails/refuses to exercise reasonable
diligence in *control* of such child -or- person knowingly acts in
manner likely to be *injurious* to physical/mental/moral welfare
of child *under* 17 or directs/authorizes to engage in *occupation*
dangerous to life/health.

Group 6: OFFENSES AGAINST JUSTICE

❏ **Absconding From Release** **Misd. - Felony**
having been released from confinement to participate in a fur-
lough, work release or temporary release program, intentionally fails to return to institution/facility at or before prescribed
time -or- leaves or fails to return to a community treatment
facility without authorization.

❏ **Bail Jumping** **Misd. - Felony**
having been released from custody or allowed to remain at
liberty upon bail or own recognizance, *fails* to appear *per-
sonally* on required date or voluntarily within *30 days* thereafter (seriousness of underlying charge determines degree of
offense).

❏ **Compounding A Crime** **Misdemeanor**
agrees/offers/confers any *benefit* upon agreement or understanding that recipient will *refrain* from initiating a prosecution
for a crime. (conversely, to agree/solicit/accept any benefit is
also unlawful).

❑ **Contempt, Criminal**   **Misd. - Felony**
intentionally disobeys/resists the lawful process or other mandate of a court -or- violates Order of Protection.

❑ **Falsely Report Incident 3°**   **Misdemeanor**
knowingly and gratuitously reports to law enforcement office/
agency: alleged past or impending occurrence of offense/inci-
dent which *did not* or is *not about to* occur -or- *false info.* re:
actual offense/incident or *implication* of some person therein.

❑ **Governmental Administration, Obstruct**   **Misd. - Felony**
intentionally obstructs/impairs/perverts administration of law
or other government function -or- attempts/prevents public
servant from performing official function by any unlawful act or
by interfering with telecommunication system owned/operated
by municipality, fire district or E.M.S. (any resulting serious
physical injury elevates degree of offense).

❑ **Order Of Protection, Violate**   **Felony**
having been *duly served* or *aware* of Order due to being in
court when issued, violator intentionally/recklessly: causes
physical/serious injury or damages subject's property exceeding $250.00 -or- disobeys *stay-away* provision, having *pre-
vious conviction* of same within preceding *5 years.*

❑ **Public Benefit Card, Use/Possession**   **Misd. - Felony**
knowingly: accepts card as *collateral* for a loan, obtains card
in exchange for a *benefit,* transfers/ delivers card in exchange
for *money or drugs* or for purpose of committing an unlawful
act. (use/ possession of multiple cards elevates degree of
offense charged).

❑ **Solicitation, Criminal 2°, 4°, 5°**   **Vio.-Misd.-Fel.**
intending that another engage in conduct constituting a *crime,*
solicits, requests, etc....or otherwise attempts to *cause* such
person to *engage* in such conduct (type of offense *solicited*
elevates degree of offense charged).

❑ **Welfare Fraud**   **Misd. - Felony**
commits a fraudulent welfare act and thereby takes/obtains
public assistance benefits (increased value of assistance elevates degree of offense charged).

Group 7: OFFENSES RE: PROPERTY / FINANCES

❑ **Arson 3° & 4°**   **Felony**
recklessly damages building/motor vehicle by *intentionally
starting* fire or causing explosion (*intent to damage* such property elevates degree of offense charged).

❑ **Checks, Issue Bad**   **Misdemeanor**
knowing there are *insufficient* funds and *intending or believing*
check will be *refused* and payment *is* in fact refused: *utters*
(as drawer or rep. drawer) or *passes* such check.

❑ **Credit/Debit/Public Benefit Card**   **Misdemeanor**
in the course of attempting/obtaining *property* or a *service:*
uses/displays a credit/debit/public benefit card which he
knows to be *revoked/canceled.*

❑ **Contempt, Criminal 1°**   **Felony**
in violation of *duly served* Order of Protection or *aware* of its
existence, having been present in court when issued, inten-
tionally/recklessly damages subjects property *exceeding*
$250.00.

❑ **Endangerment, Reckless**   **Misdemeanor**
recklessly engages in conduct which creates *substantial risk*
of damage to another's property *exceeding* $250.00.

❑ **Financial Statement, False**   **Felony**
with intent to *defraud*, knowingly makes/utters written instrument describing *financial condition* or *ability to pay* which is
materially inaccurate -or- falsely *represents* in writing that such
instrument is *accurate.*

❑ **Forged Instrument, Criminal Poss. of**   **Misd. - Felony**
knowingly and with *intent* to defraud, deceives or injure
another: *utters/possesses* a forged instrument (deed, will,

codicil, contract, credit card, public record, securities, stocks, bonds, etc. elevate degree of offense charged).

❏ **Forgery**   **Misd. - Felony**
with *intent* to defraud, deceive or injure another: falsely makes, completes or alters a written instrument. (type of instrument elevates degree of offense charged).

❏ **Larceny, Grand**   **Felony**
with *intent* to deprive or appropriate to self/3rd person, *wrongfully* takes/obtains/withholds property from another (value and type of property determines degree of offense charged).

❏ **Larceny, Petit**   **Misdemeanor**
steals property: personal/real, money, computer data/program, thing of value, etc. up to $1,000 in value.

❏ **Misapplication of Property**   **Misdemeanor**
knowingly possessing another's personal property pursuant to *agreement* that it be *returned* at future time: loans/leases/pawns or otherwise encumbers *without consent* and *creating risk* that owner will be *unable* to recover property or suffer pecuniary *loss*.

❏ **Mischief, Criminal**   **Misd. - Felony**
having no right to do so nor reasonable ground to so believe, damages another's property: *intentionally* (use of explosive or value of property determines degree of offense charged) -or- *recklessly* (value over $250.00).

❏ **Stolen Property, Possession of**   **Misd. - Felony**
knowingly possesses stolen property with *intent* to *benefit* self/another or *impede recovery* by owner. (type of or value of property determines degree of offense charged).

❏ **Tampering, Criminal 3°**   **Misdemeanor**
having *no right* to do so nor reasonable ground to so believe, tampers with another's property with *intent* to cause *substantial inconvenience* to victim/3rd person.

❑ **Vehicle, Unauthorized Use of** Misd. - Felony
knowingly takes, operates, exercises control over, rides in or
otherwise uses vehicle without owner's consent (previous
conviction or intent to use vehicle re: commission/flight from
certain felonies shall elevate degree of offense charged).

❑ **Victim/Witness, Intimidate 3°** Felony
knowing another *possesses information* re: criminal trans-
action, *intentionally* damages property of such person/another
to compel *refraining* to communicate with authorities or in
retaliation for such communication.

❑ **Will, Unlawfully Conceal** Felony
with intent to defraud: conceals/secretes/suppresses/muti-
lates/destroys a will, codicil or other testamentary instrument.

TABULATION

Has your partner broken the law? If so, to what extent and
how often? Maybe it's not as bad as you thought. Maybe it's
worse. Since these results can provide a behavioral *profile* of your
partner, they will come in handy during the *assessment* process.
Once you've analyzed *his* criminal activities, you'll have a better
idea of where *you* stand.

Keep *tabs* on his unlawful activities and inclinations. If the
picture looks bleak, *share* the results of this section with your
counselor, your attorney, your confidant. Anyone with your best
interests in mind, will recommend some form of INTERVENTION.

FOR CONSIDERATION

Our elected representatives have the means to poll their
constituents, solicit opinions, evaluate recommendations, form
committees, conduct hearings, research data, analyze results,
study proposals, consider alternatives, and ultimately draft
legislation affecting a wide range of human behavior.

Because acts of domestic violence come within their legislative scope of authority, laws, policies and procedures regulating the prevention, punishment and treatment thereof must be periodically reviewed and amended to keep abreast of prevalent societal conditions.

FORMULA FOR ACTION

Victim's Outrage + Advocacy Pressure + Public Awareness + Media Attention = Legislative Response. That's the way it should work. If this formula is not working, your representatives are pre-occupied and need a good nudge.

FOOD FOR THOUGHT

- Fine-tune *existing* laws and procedures.

- Upgrade penalties for assaults upon *pregnant* females.

- Set *strict* sentencing guidelines for serious and/or repeated acts of violence.

- Prohibit persons named in an Order of Protection from purchasing or owning a *firearm*.

- Create a *separate* criminal offense for acts of domestic violence.

- Require the reporting of cases of *suspected* spousal abuse to a central registry using the suspected child abuse procedure and apparatus as a model.

SAFETY NET

In order to better aid victims of domestic violence (especially the indigent) legislators should establish, maintain or increase the following:

◘ Shelters; should be safe, secure and protessionally staffed.

◘ Medical programs; for victims and children.

◘ Welfare programs; to provide temporary relief.

◘ Food stamps; for temporary and necessary sustinence.

◘ AFDC; for aid to families with dependent children.

◘ Transportation services; to and from shelters, court hearings, employment opportunities, etc.

◘ Counseling; to provide referrals at least, actual services at best.

◘ Miscellaneous; provide appropriations for such things as Victim's Advocate Programs, Victim's Assistance Programs, Volunteer Assistance Programs, Police Response Grants and experimental programs designed to aid the victim directly or indirectly.

Legislators should be aware that inadequate or non-existent programs will often *deter* the victim from leaving a violent home. Removing or reducing programs already in place is tantamount to confining the victims to their abusive dwelling.

This page intentionally left blank.

Part 2 - C

ORIGINATION

Y ou will need to know *how* to originate a domestic/family proceeding in the court system.

Some victims can find their way into and around the system even if they were blindfolded. The victim who is new to the domestic violence scene however, will say: What do I do? How do I go about this? Where do I go from here? Who takes care of this?

Note that a *family court* proceeding is generally a *civil* proceeding and is for the *purpose* of attempting to stop the violence, end the family disruption and obtain protection for the victims.

A *criminal* court proceeding on the other hand, is for the purpose of *prosecuting* the offender and can result in a *criminal* conviction of the offender.

PROCEDURAL QUESTIONS

The following questions, categorized by function and procedure, should be addressed to your legal counsel or victim's advocate. Their responses should assist you in gaining better insight into the mechanics of originating a family court proceeding.

■ PRE-FILING

❏ Is my allegation *worthy* of the court's time and attention?

❏ Must an *arrest* take place *before* I can file and/or apply for court intervention?

❏ Must an incident be *reported* to the police before filing with the court?

❏ Which court (family, criminal, other) has *jurisdiction* over my domestic / family situation?

❏ Shall the court(s) have concurrent or exclusive jurisdiction?

❏ Will I be instituting a civil or criminal action with the court?

❏ Who do I notify if I am discouraged or prevented from filing a petition with the court?

❏ Can a relative initiate a court action on my behalf if for some reason I cannot?

❏ What services and referrals are available through the court?

■ FILING

❏ Do I file in the county where I reside or where the abuser resides, if not the same?

❏ Specifically, *where* do I go to file / apply for court relief?

❏ Will court personnel *assist* me in the filing or application phase?

❏ What are the filing fees, if any?

❏ What information, records or documents must I bring or have at my disposal when filing?

■ PRE-HEARING

❏ Will my partner receive a summons or notice to appear?

❏ What if he fails or refuses to appear as directed?

❏ How soon will it take to get my case heard?

❏ Will my partner be arrested?

❏ May I address the court before my partner is *released* on recognizance or bail is set?

❏ Must I speak with the defense counsel if I am approached prior to the court hearing or trial?

❏ Who do I notify if I discover that my partner has left the jurisdiction?

❏ Will a *translator* be available for non-English speaking parties in the proceeding?

❏ May I request that a non-witness friend, relative, advisor or social worker be *present* in the court room or chambers?

❏ Is my partner permitted to make a similar request?

❏ How will I be notified of a hearing date?

■ HEARING

❏ To what extent must the allegation against my partner be substantiated?

❏ Are the court proceedings held in closed session or are they open to the public?

❏ What are my rights?

❏ At what point can I request temporary spousal and/or child support through the court?

❏ Can I obtain a temporary Order of Protection?

❏ How do I answer a counter-charge?

❏ Will I need legal *representation*?

❏ May I request an adjournment in order to consult with an attorney?

❏ If I am unable to afford counsel, am I entitled to representation as an indigent?

❏ Who do I *notify* if I am *harassed* by my partner or an intermediary while the case is being processed?

❏ How do I pursue restitution for losses sustained as a result of my partner's behavior?

❏ What if I want to reconcile with my partner?

❏ Must I submit to a reconciliation proceeding?

■ POST-HEARING

❏ If my petition is dismissed, what recourse do I have, if any?

❏ Are records, reports and orders emanating from the proceedings confidential or available to the public?

❏ Who do I *notify* if there is a *violation* of a court order?

Chapter Three

HELP AVAILABLE

❏ Part 3 - A   PROTECTION

❏ Part 3 - B   INTERVENTION

❏ Part 3 - C   REPRESENTATION

This page intentionally left blank.

Part 3 - A

PROTECTION

Battered women are getting fed up with their mates, their life-style and the systemic factors which seem to perpetuate their cycle of misery. But things are beginning to show signs of improvement.

More and more victims of domestic violence seem willing to ask for help....especially when *encouraged* by family, friends and co-workers. More victims are willing to ask for protection and put their faith in the "system."

To help enlighten you on court-sponsored procedures for protection, this portion of the Domestic Violence Survival Guide will deal exclusively with Orders of Protection....what they are, what they do and how to get them.

GENERAL DEFINITION

In our discussion of court-ordered protection, the Order of Protection, Restraining Order and Domestic Violence Injunction can be used interchangeably. These documents generally *require* compliance with specific conditions of behavior, hours of visitation and any other condition deemed appropriate by the court of issuance.

Precise definitions will vary among different jurisdictions.

An Order of Protection may also be issued as part of a separation decree, divorce judgment, annulment or as part of a court order in a *pending* separation, divorce or annulment action.

USE OF TERMS

Note that the terms "petitioner" and "respondent" pertain to Family Offense Proceedings. The terms "complainant" and "defendant" pertain to criminal proceedings.

Orders of Protection and temporary Orders of Protection are commonly available in *both* instances.

BASIS FOR ISSUANCE

The procedures and guidelines concerning the issuance of Orders of Protection are governed by appropriate state law.

In fairness to all parties concerned, an Order of Protection should not be requested or issued on a whim. The frequency, severity, pattern and consequences of past abuse....coupled with the likelihood of danger of future abuse upon the partner or family member....should aid the court in determining the necessity for such an order.

UPON ISSUANCE

Upon obtaining an Order of Protection, it is recommended that you visit your local police station. Attempt to *meet* with the domestic violence *specialist* and provide *background* information as to *why* the Order was issued.

Laying this groundwork may assist officers responding to sub-sequent 9-1-1 calls in that they will be *familiar* with your situation and thus be able to act quickly and effectively.

RESTRICTIONS

Typical restrictive clauses *may* include one or more of the following:

■ BEHAVIORAL

❏ Stay-away from residence, place of employment, business, school, etc. (possibly with *or* without further conditions attached).

❏ Permit the removal of undisputed personal belongings from the residence at or during a designated time period.

■ RE: CHILD/OTHERS

❏ Restrict *visitation* by a parent or stipulated person to certain time and places.

❏ Forbid the commission of a criminal offense against the child....or any family or household member....or any person who has custody of the child.

❏ Refrain from acts of commission or omission which create unreasonable risk to the health, safety or welfare of a child, family or household member's life or health.

■ ECONOMIC

❏ Require the payment of certain costs and fees incurred to obtain or enforce the order.

❏ Reimburse the petitioner for expenses incurred for medical care and treatment arising from the domestic incident.

■ REHABILITATIVE

❏ Require participation in a batterer's education program.

❏ Require participation in a drug/alcohol counseling program.

❏ Cooperate with the court and intervention services to further the purposes of protection.

MECHANICS

If you are new to the world of domestic violence...inexperienced with the "system" designed to control it....unaware of the capabilities and limitations of orders of protection....you will have *questions* which must be put to your attorney, victim's advocate, police representative, intervention specialist, etc.

Suggested areas of *inquiry* have been grouped into five basic categories as follows:

■ FILING

▣ What section of *law* governs the filing and processing of an Order of Protection?

▣ Who may file a *petition* for obtaining a protection order?

▣ When may the *respondent* file an *answer* to the petition?

■ PROCEDURAL

▣ How do I go about *amending* or *modifying* an existing Order?

▣ Under what circumstances, if any, can an Order be *revoked?*

▣ Is this the appropriate time to address the issue of *custody?*

■ Can an Order for temporary *child support* be issued in conjunction with a temporary Order of Protection?

■ Can employer-provided *medical* coverage, where applicable, be *included* as part of an Order of temporary support?

■ TECHNICAL

■ Is the issuance of an Order of Protection tantamount to a finding of wrongdoing by the court?

■ How long shall the Order remain in effect?

■ Can *addresses* be kept *confidential*, if not already known to the parties concerned?

■ Will the respondent's *counter-claim* be heard on the same day as the return date set for the original petition?

■ Will a *copy* of the Order be on file with the local *police* department?

■ Shall the details of the Order be accessible via a state-wide *computer* hook-up?

■ SERVICE

■ When may an Order of Protection be served (i.e., day of week, hour of day or night)?

■ Who may serve an Order (i.e., police officer, peace officer, other person)?

■ Where may such service take place?

■ What criteria shall constitute *proof* of service?

◼ May the officer or person designated to serve the Order be held *liable* for damages resulting from any *failure* to achieve lawful service?

■ VIOLATIONS

◼ Who do I *notify* when there is an apparent violation of the Order of Protection?

◼ What procedural steps occur after the court is made aware of a violation?

◼ What are the criminal *sanctions* for violating an Order?

◼ Depending upon the violation, may or must the court *order* the surrender of any licensed *firearms* possessed by the respondent?

LIMITATIONS

When discussing the use of an Order of Protection as a *protective* device, a reality check is in order.

IS VS. IS NOT

At the risk of creating a sense of futility, it must be emphasized that an Order of Protection is in point of fact, a piece of *paper*....not an iron cocoon to embrace and defend you against a clenched fist or a deadly weapon.

True, the order is not *just* a piece of paper....it has *legal* and *judicial* significance, just as the subscribing judge intended when he drafted and signed it. But, the order is only as impressive and deterring as the respondent *allows* it to be.

An angry or resentful individual will *not* be dissuaded from exacting *his* form of "justice" if he is sufficiently motivated and *determined* to harm you.

Many victims have been severely injured and even killed with an Order of Protection in their handbag or clutched in their hands.

THE ROAD TO TRAVEL

Harsh reality is *not* intended to discourage you from taking the Order of Protection route. Short of having armed guards at your side 24 hours a day, you must avail yourself of *all* lawful avenues open to you, including relocation and change of identity, if such *extreme* measures are deemed *appropriate*.

THE PRIMARY ROUTES

Awareness:
- ▶ Be aware of his potential.
- ▶ Be conscious of your vulnerability.
- ▶ Be alert to your surroundings.
- ▶ Be vigilant at all times.

Thinking:
- ▶ Think posltlvely.
- ▶ Think realistically.
- ▶ Think constructively.
- ▶ Think strategically.

Planning:
- ▶ Plan for an attack.
- ▶ Plan for an escape.
- ▶ Plan for taking refuge.
- ▶ Plan for a worst case scenario.

This page intentionally left blank.

Part 3 - B

INTERVENTION

N o one deserves to be beaten and no one should have to tolerate such abuse. Though either party is *capable* of provoking frustration and anger in the other, this should *not* cause or justify physical abuse.

When the first violent act occurs, it is usually shocking, sometimes to both parties. Being an "aberration," it won't ever happen again, especially since he is so very, very sorry.

After a lull, it happens again, but this time you "deserved it." By now though, you've fallen in love with him because of his positive, charming qualities. Seems that you're hooked, maybe even trapped.

As the relationship solidifies, the abuse increases. By now, you learn to cope because of the advantages inherent in the relationship. So, you begin to make excuses for him (i.e., his job, his boss, his health, his bad luck, his ex-wife, etc.) You believe you can help him.

But things go from bad to worse. Now he is threatening everybody: you, your relatives, your children. Ridiculing you is not enough. He must punch you to drive home his point. After he's beaten you and caused scars and bruises, you become "ugly."

Time passes and you change. You become evasive, not showing your strong or real feelings. You're frightened, preferring to placate your partner rather than provoke him. You're protective of him, demonstrating loyalty, so he won't retaliate for your independence and disobedience. But this is not really you. You are exercising survival strategies and doing your best to cope.

But how long can you hold out without help? Perhaps you're ready for INTERVENTION.

Q. With your partner blaming you for all the problems in the home, with your friends and family blaming you for not leaving and with society blaming you for your dilemma, how can you possibly overcome?

A. Intervention! Counseling! Therapy!

It is far easier for the abuser to blame the partner for being less than perfect than for the abuser to take responsibility for the resulting but unwarranted abuse.

It is far easier for your friends and family to tell you to just leave than for them to contemplate the ramifications of such a move.

It is far easier for society to shrug their collective shoulders than to understand the dynamics of the abusive relationship.

"Why does she stay?" must become "Why does he *beat* her?" followed by "How can we get him to *stop*?"

New relationships straying into abusive territory seldom solicit outside intervention. It is usually when the victim discovers that she is "lost" and without a "compass" that she seeks guidance. Such guidance usually comes from a friend, relative or neighbor who has "been there." Their advice and experience may lend some moral support, at least temporarily. But the potential for doing more harm than good, must be considered.

It is the **established relationship** that usually cries out for professional intervention in the form of police response and victim's shelters initially; and counseling and therapy down the road.

BEFORE VS. AFTER

Sometimes, intervention is *forced* upon a victim (i.e., when the neighbors call the police or when emergency room treatment becomes necessary). The *ideal* situation is for the victim to take a pro-active stance and minimize the risk of physical injury to herself and her children.

PRO-ACTIVE DETERRENT VALUE

Acceptance - women who receive counseling and/or support services are *less* likely to accept abuse from their *current* partner or to choose *another* abusive partner.

Escalation - without early intervention, domestic violence can escalate in severity and lead to *murder*, the ultimate expression of the batterer's need to control.

Homicide - there seems to be a correlation between an *increase* in legal protection and services for battered women -and- a *decrease* in the number of homicides committed by *women* against their male partners.

POST- ACTIVE DETERRENT VALUE

Police Calls - studies have shown that calling the police following an abusive act *reduces* the risk of another attack within six months by more than 50%.

Police Action - arresting the abuser appears to *reduce* recidivism, even if the arrest does not result in a conviction.

Reversal - with proper intervention, batterers can *discover* their excessive needs for power and control and *learn* more appropriate and acceptable responses.

"ASK AND I'LL TELL"

Many victims seem reluctant to *volunteer* personal information about their domestic situation. But if *asked*....by health professionals, for example....about what appears to be signs of physical or sexual abuse, many victims will welcome such expressions of concern and avail themselves of the *opportunity* to unload their burden. This can be a start.

FOUR-STEP PROCESS

Proper intervention is not a one-shot deal. Effective results are best achieved by a four-step, coordinated approach:

❶ **POLICE PRO-ARREST POLICY:** a no nonsense philosophy sets the stage for action; this initial intervention can provide *immediate* aid and comfort to the victim.

❷ **PROSECUTION FOLLOW-THROUGH:** as the "ball" goes into the prosecutor's court, the judge acts as referee....calling for "time out" and penalties.

❸ **FOLLOW-UP SUPPORT:** appropriate public and private agencies are notified and brought into the picture to *help* the abused person.

❹ **INTERVENTION PROGRAM:** subsequent intervention now provides a means of helping the *abuser* to control his *anger*, not his partner.

BENEFITS GALORE

The interaction of these four components can help accomplish the following major objectives:

✔ Relieve the victim of the difficult burden of deciding whether or not to pursue a court action.

✔ Punish the abuser when deemed appropriate.

✔ Alter abusive/violent behavior.

✔ Restore tranquility to the home.

ACCOUNTABILITY

The *escalation* of violence is the *means* to an *end;* that end is *power and control* over the victim. Understanding this concept is vital to ensuring effective intervention. Because violent behavior is a *choice* based on the abuser's *belief* in the *right* to *dominate* the relationship, intervention must hold the abuser *accountable* and impose *consequences* for such behavior.

Conversely, intervention which addresses domestic violence as behavior over which the abuser has little control, will do precious *little* to hold the abuser *accountable* and may do additional *harm* by further *endangering* the victim.

POLICE INTERVENTION

Since the "entertainment" industry provides us with more frequent and more graphic violence, how can the recipient of a "little slapping around" from a domestic disagreement, expect to be taken seriously by society in general and by the police in particular?

As morals continue to decline....as the concept of family values is ridiculed by the "hip" comedians and social commentators....how can the "alleged victim" of physical or sexual assault dare to make a formal complaint against her "lover?"

Society in general and the legal system in particular has traditionally been *reluctant* to intervene in family matters, especially *after* violence has occurred. Though the act is illegal, and the behavior is unpleasant, the nature of the continuing relationship....with its inherent *emotional ties* and actual or *quasi-family structure*....often cause the victim to, in effect, *join* with society and the "system" to become *ambivalent* about sending "Daddy" off to prison.

Consequently, there has been a bias toward keeping the family together....at all costs. The "system" was customarily more eager to prosecute the mugger or the burglar than some guy who came home from work, found that his dinner wasn't ready and smacked his wife around to vent his anger.

Due to the increased public awareness of domestic violence in the 1970's, law enforcement agencies came under increased pressure to intervene. Communities began to establish emergency shelters, counseling programs, support services and in some areas, counseling programs for the *abusers.*

Though policies were changed and procedures were modified, attitudes have taken the slow track in focusing on the batterer as a *law breaker.*

FORMER THINKING

The past attitudes of the police have reflected the general attitude held by society....that of non-intervention....that *most* domestic incidents, except those involving serious injury or death, were a private, family matter and not of concern to the police. Offenders were coaxed to "cool off" and were seldom arrested. Victims received sympathy, but minimal protection.

NEW THINKING

Fortunately, a new trend is emerging. Non-intervention is becoming the exception rather than the rule. Police departments and the "system" have begun to take a firmer stand against domestic violence. A tendency toward the arrest and prosecution of offenders has evolved but still needs improvement in some jurisdictions.

OPERATING PHILOSOPHY

The new working policy for the official and on-going response to domestic violence should be guided primarily by the *nature* of the abusive act and *not* the *relationship* between the abused and the abuser. No longer considered a private, family matter, assault is a *criminal* offense. Tolerance must be reduced to zero!

POLICE RESPONSE

The police customarily respond when the abuse gets physical, out of control or crosses the threshold into the violent stage. Police intervention is probably the most common, most frequently utilized form of assistance available. Everyone, including many children, know their number: 9-1-1. But even a call to the police can be fraught with apprehension. What do I say? Will they come? Will they help? And scariest of all: what happens after they leave?

MAKING THE CALL

The purpose of the call is to report unlawful activity which has *just* taken place, is *now* taking place or is *about* to take place and to request the presence of the police and/or ambulance for yourself or another person.

Once you've decided to make the call, do it right.

- ◉ Speak clearly and in a controlled, conversational tone of voice; yelling and screaming will *not* hasten police arrival.

- ◉ Give your name, street address, apartment number, floor number, room number, whether front, side or rear entrance, etc.

- ◉ State exactly what is happening *now* or has *just* taken place; if you have *reason* to believe something is about to happen, state so and why.

- ◉ Indicate whether or not your partner is holding or has ready access to a *weapon*; if so, describe the weapon.

- ◉ Inform the police operator whether you have a current Order of Protection.

- Request the operator's name and/or I.D. number; make a record of same along with the time you called.

WHILE WAITING

- Realize that many police agencies are short-staffed and over-worked; delays in patrol response are often routine in some jurisdictions.

- Do your best to keep calm; don't get brave and aggressive now that the police are coming.

- Refrain from further discussion and argument if possible; if he has calmed down or fallen asleep take advantage of the opportunity to collect your thoughts (and belongings if you subsequently decide to leave).

UPON ARRIVAL

- Try to remain calm, rational and helpful; the responding officers need *information*, not undue hysteria.

- Explain why you requested police intervention; make your case and then let the police do their job.

- Do not acquire false courage and assault your partner in front of the officers; succumbing to this temptation would be counter-productive.

POLICE ACTION

The police are now standing in your living room. What should you expect at this point?

◼ Professional appearance and demeanor.

◼ Concern for the needs of any person requiring immediate *medical* attention.

◼ Sensitivity and an objective frame of mind.

◼ Knowledge of pertinent criminal and family *laws.*

◼ Initiative to take relevant notes and record evidence.

◼ Compliance with departmental policy and regulations relating to domestic violence.

◼ Making arrests where appropriate.

Police intervention should never be indifferent. Officers should never minimize the seriousness of an assault nor hesitate to interfere in another man's home, nor fail to act out of unwarranted fear of physical confrontation.

EXPECTATIONS

Sometimes, expectations are high....too high and downright *illegal.* The police *cannot* break the law, violate department regulations or deny one's civil rights in order to satisfy *your* immediate desires.

Matters relating to negligence, invasion of privacy, unlawful use of force, denial of due process, false arrest, etc. are (or should be) uppermost on the minds of all police officers. As a result, there are (or should be) *limitations* on just how far an officer can go to remedy your situation.

If for example, your partner has *not* committed a violation of law and co-owns or co-rents the dwelling with you, he *cannot* be "thrown out" because he's been drinking and is now argumentative.

Police officers must act with "objective legal reasonableness" when enforcing criminal laws. Common sense, fairness and impartiality are required when dealing with others.

In addition to state criminal charges and departmental disciplinary sanctions which the officer may face, the *willful* violation of a person's federal civil rights can result in criminal prosecution by the U.S. Department of Justice under Title 18, Section 241 and 242 of the United States Code. Sound serious? It is!

If you are in doubt or have any specific questions as to exactly what your local police can do, cannot do, may do and must do in a particular domestic situation, clarify any unresolved issues with a reliable source (i.e., Domestic Violence Specialist, Community Affairs Officer, Supervising Officer, Precinct Commander, Department Legal Section, Municipal Attorney's Office, etc.)

If you needed a loan you wouldn't go into a bank and expect details and specifics from a teller. You'd go to the loan officer or branch manager. The same applies to seeking help on a domestic matter.

Go to the "specialist" at your local police precinct or station house. Ask *specific* questions of the police officer or detective assigned to domestic violence cases and make *notes*. Ask for the *name,* and rank or title of the person with whom you are speaking. This should prompt the spokesperson to be as helpful and as accurate as possible.

MEDICAL ATTENTION

As a victim, you must *inform* medical personnel that your injuries are a *result* of domestic violence and request *documentation* of your visit.

Hospital emergency departments should have *protocols* in place to *routinely* identify, treat and refer victims of domestic abuse and sexual assault to the appropriate agencies.

COMMON MISCONCEPTION

Do the police have a *duty* to protect not just the public in general, but also the *individual?*

Not necessarily! Where the doctrines of "Sovereign Immunity" and "Duty at Large" are applicable, the police are *protected* from a finding of liability.

Such findings are the exception, rather than the rule. The courts are extremely *reluctant* to find liability for the commission of a crime and the Police Department's failure to prevent it.

Civil actions such as, failure to protect, failure to respond to calls for assistance, failure to arrest or restrain dangerous persons, failure to protect persons brought into contact with assailants and failure to investigate, are *not* the open and shut type cases that you might otherwise imagine.

PRIMARY INTERVENTION SOURCES

The police alone *cannot* stop domestic violence. There must be a coordinated and cooperative effort on the part of numerous agencies, entities and individuals.

The following list presents some of the **primary** sources of assistance for the victims of domestic abuse:

POLICE DEPARTMENTS - your local police department should be prepared to send *knowledgeable* officers, *well-trained* in domestic violence matters, who are *sensitive* to the problems and needs of victims.

POLICE OFFICERS - are on duty around the clock to serve and protect. No other agency is as available, on a continuous basis, to respond right to your *doorstep*.

LOCAL HOT LINE - your local domestic violence hot line is your *direct* link to community-based assistance. It should be used to speak with a counselor for *guidance* and *encouragement* and for direction to the nearest *shelter* or safe house.

NATIONAL HOT LINE - the national hot line provides *confidential* crisis intervention, counseling, information, referrals and a direct connection to valuable sources of help. Because the call is toll-free, no record of the call will appear on your phone bill. **(1-800/799-7233)**

THE "SYSTEM" - rather than think of it as a nameless, faceless, non-entity, *learn* about it, *discover* how it works and *meet* the players as they work to keep *you* from falling between the proverbial cracks.

VICTIMS ADVOCATES - check with your local police department and district attorney's office to ascertain if such a program is available in your community. If so, *utilize* this *valuable* service. As they walk you through the "system," they'll support, inform, explain, refer and encourage you in your time of critical need.

COURTS - are the foundation of the Criminal Justice System and society's instrument for holding people *accountable* for their unlawful acts.

PROSECUTORS - the "lubricant" which oils the gears of the System, they move the offender from the point of arrest to the courtroom for a momentous meeting with judge and jury.

JUDGES - play a major role in *deterring* and *controlling* domestic violence. Their ability to provide Orders of Protection for the victim; coupled with their *latitude* and *discretionary* powers in dealing with the offenders, enable them to *make* the "system" work.

JURIES - an *integral* part of the "system," they must perform their jury duty as the *judge* instructs and, as society's collective conscience, *remove* any bias in favor of a person's "right" to *control* their partner and family.

MEDICAL PROFESSION - family and personal physicians, public health doctors and emergency room attendants should be on the *alert* for *signs* of domestic abuse. Referrals and literature should be made available for those acknowledging or obviously being subjected to domestic abuse.

SOCIAL SERVICE AGENCIES - your local public agencies providing welfare benefits and social services can offer vital information and support on matters relating to victim's services, temporary housing, emergency funds, specialized counseling, legal matters, etc. Avail yourself!

SECONDARY SOURCES

The following list presents **secondary** sources of assistance to the victims of domestic abuse.

GOVERNMENT AGENCIES - various agencies of the state government can provide assistance with matters which often arise as a result of domestic disturbances.

For example: Education Dept. = G.E.D. preparation, adult education courses, etc.; Labor Dept. = employment opportunities, placement preparation, etc.; Health Dept. = physical, mental or emotional evaluation, family counseling and substance abuse programs, etc.

STATE COALITIONS - in addition to the National Coalition Against Domestic Violence, each of the 50 states have a state-wide coalition of victims, former victims, activist groups, professional organizations, private citizens, and other interested parties, working together in an activist-supportive mode in the battle against domestic violence.

Annual membership fees are generally modest and affordable. Benefits may differ among the various coalitions but generally include the issuance of bulletins and newsletters, access to resource and reference manuals, information and referral services, participation in forums and seminars and other membership services.

Current addresses and phone numbers may be obtained from your local shelter or victim's group.

If your abuser has access to your mail delivery, you may want to use a post office box or have personal mail of this nature delivered in care of a close friend, neighbor or relative.

PUBLIC SERVICE ORGANIZATIONS - such as United Way and the Salvation Army can and should be called upon for information and referral initially and outreach services where available. Inquire!

SPECIALIZED HELP ORGANIZATIONS - highly successful organizations dealing in alcohol and substance abuse are at your disposal. Alcoholics Anonymous provides support groups for people who wish to stop drinking. Al-Anon aids their *adult* family members and Ala-teen aids their *teenage* family members. These fellowships share experiences, strength and hope in order to help solve their common problems.

Narcotics Anonymous is fashioned like A.A. but specializes in assisting those with a dependence on addictive drugs. Look up these fine organizations in your telephone directory.

LEGAL PROFESSION - contact the county Bar Association for a list of attorneys in your area who specialize in Family Law. If finances are a problem, inquire if any listed attorneys charge on a sliding scale or "pro bono publico," a Latin term meaning "for the public welfare" (more literal translation: without charge). If so, ascertain the criteria for participation in such a program.

Organizations such as the Legal Aid Society are more apt to represent the abuser than the abused in a criminal charge. You can call them though as part of the "networking" procedure.

RELIGIOUS COMMUNITY - each religion, each denomination and each church or synagogue *may* offer a service or program for victims of domestic abuse. Any such services will *vary* depending upon the organization's philosophy and availability of funds, personnel and other resources. The large religious organizations known for charity work, should be called upon for information, assistance or referral.

SCHOOL SYSTEM - in addition to their many duties, teachers and school officials are asked to be on the lookout for signs of abuse in their students. Preliminary counseling should be accessible for those students in need. Issues relating to residing in an abusive home should be incorporated into the school program. Discussion of the topic should be available to all students.

Abusive home life has a direct affect upon academic performance. For the sake of the child, any obvious or suspected problem should be addressed in a professional setting at a parent-teacher conference. Information, literature and referrals should be on hand as may be appropriate.

FRIENDS/FAMILIES - this group, including *trusted* neighbors and co-workers, are often the *first* to be called upon to provide aid and comfort. Their help though valuable, is *not* comparable to that available from a trained, skilled and experienced counselor or therapist.

In addition to this, their help is often *temporary* as they tend to lose patience with the on-going exploits of the batterer as he keeps the cycle of violence in perpetual motion. If the *victim* fails to work towards ending that cycle, patience depletes even faster.

VICTIMS - finally there is the victim herself. You are the ultimate source of intervention. You must *want* help; you must *seek* help; you must *accept* help. The *alternative* is just *more* of the *same* and you deserve *better!*

INDIRECT INTERVENTION

The following list presents various indirect avenues of assistance...some tangible, some more abstract....but nonetheless ultimately beneficial in the struggle against domestic violence.

These sources tend to answer the question: "How can *we* help *you*?"

LEGISLATORS - must help to *reduce* the incidence and severity of domestic violence, *prevent* future incidents and *protect* victims with necessary support services via strong *legislation* and adequate *funding* for pertinent agencies and programs.

Strong legislation, without adequate funding, is like having a fine set of architectural drawings but no money to build with. Write your legislative representatives to offer your suggestions, comments and concerns in matters relating to domestic violence.

CITIZENS - must be *aware* of, *concerned* about and *supportive* of domestic abuse issues within their community. If their home is free of domestic violence they should consider themselves *blessed*, not indifferent to the plight of others around them. Sooner or later, one way or another, domestic violence will affect us all.

COMMUNITY COALITION - a union of concerned citizens and community organizations can be formed to help influence outcomes or goals on the domestic violence problem. A *coalition* can accomplish a wide range of goals which reach *beyond* the capacity of any *individual* member. Goals can *range* from the sharing of information to the coordination of services; from community education to advocacy for major policy or regulatory changes.

VOLUNTEER GROUPS - volunteers can do baby-sitting, cradle-rocking, story-telling, meal-preparing, telephone-answering, clerical-assisting and morale-building at the local women's shelter. Senior citizens have many areas of *expertise* which can be of value in the community's effort to aid victims of abuse.

Volunteer and community groups should explore the concept of "adopting" a victim of violence. We adopt highways, so why not a neighbor in need?

MISCELLANEOUS GROUPS - local organizations of a social, fraternal, professional, neighborhood or civic nature can and should "get involved" in the domestic abuse occurring in their community. This can best be accomplished through fundraising drives, public awareness campaigns, volunteer efforts and advocacy programs....all aimed at helping the victim and their families.

BUSINESS COMMUNITY - in general, they can apply their commercial specialty in an area where it best fits the need. In particular, they can aid victims in shelters by setting up *drop-off* points for *donations* of clothing, canned goods, small appliances, toiletries, etc.; placing cash contribution canisters on their counters; making information bulletins available for distribution, etc.

MEDIA - the print and broadcast media have an excellent opportunity to raise public awareness, stimulate community concern, prod public officials and engage in various initiatives through public service announcements, editorials and feature news stories. For the sake of the community in general and the victims in particular, this opportunity should not be missed.

ENTERTAINMENT INDUSTRY - comedy, lyric, script and screen writers should be cognizant of the detrimental impact of trivializing, minimizing, satirizing or otherwise finding humor or entertainment value in domestic abuse, lest their audience becomes numb to the consequences.

TYPES OF NEEDS

Check the boxes on *initial* needs which may apply to you and your particular situation, upon or soon after *separation*.... things to do, things to acquire and things to look into. Use the line following each item to jot down pertinent phone numbers or other relevant information.

■ **HOUSING**
❏ Temporary Shelter _____
❏ Furniture in Storage _____
❏ Child Care _____

■ **FINANCIAL**
❑ Emergency Funds _____
❑ Food Stamps _____
❑ Budget, Prepare _____
❑ Attorney Retainer _____
❑ Unemploy. Benefits _____
❑ Disability Benefits _____
❑ Veteran's Benefits _____
❑ Social Security/SSI _____

■ **PERSONAL**
❑ Employment _____
❑ Spiritual _____
❑ Safe Dep. Box, Open _____
❑ Documents, Safeguard _____

■ **HEALTH**
❑ Physical _____
❑ Mental _____
❑ Emotional _____

■ **LEGAL**
❑ Order of Protection _____
❑ Separation Proceeding _____
❑ Paternity Suit _____
❑ Temp. Child Support _____
❑ Visitation _____
❑ Temporary Alimony _____

TYPES OF SUPPORT

■ COUNSELING
- ☐ Domestic Victimization
- ☐ Stress/Anxiety
- ☐ Depression
- ☐ Assertiveness Training
- ☐ Personal Development
- ☐ Debt/Credit
- ☐ Job Training

■ ABUSER PROGRAMS
- ☐ Anger Management
- ☐ Conflict Management
- ☐ Behavior Modification
- ☐ Alcohol Abuse
- ☐ Substance Abuse
- ☐ Parenting Classes
- ☐ Education Assistance

■ THERAPY
- ☐ Physical Therapy
- ☐ Psychotherapy
- ☐ Sex Abuse Recovery

■ FAMILY PROGRAMS
- ☐ Crisis Intervention
- ☐ Family Counseling
- ☐ Marriage Counseling

THERAPY FORMATS

 Group: benefit from the experience of others who have gone through the same ordeal. Attend community seminars and workshops and know that you are not alone.

 One-On-One: to receive the *undivided* attention of a trained professional who can zero in on *your* particular domestic situation.

Joint: batterers tend to project a significant amount of blame on their partners. Therefore, the concept of joint therapy is *controversial* in that it can *imply* that one party is partially responsible for the violence of the other. In any event, professionals urge all victims to seek counseling *themselves* if they cannot get their partners to attend.

RESOURCES

What you need is information, suggestions, options and guidance. Seek it out and avail yourself of all the help you can get. Support is available at many public and private agencies; one, some or all of which may pertain to any given abusive relationship.

Keep in mind that *multiple* interventions are often necessary. What works for one victim or offender may not work for another, regardless of any similarities in the case.

Unsuccessful results the first time out, requires a *different* approach, *not* resignation to failure.

PICK & CHOOSE

Having scanned the preceding lists of *needs* and *support* programs, determine which one(s) apply to your personal situation. Use the **Information & Referral** section to help locate and make contact with the appropriate agency.

NETWORKING

Utilize a "networking" system...."the making of contacts and trading of information"....in order to zero in on the resource(s) that will benefit you and your family. If one agency cannot assist you, they may be able to put you in touch with the one that can. Keep "networking" until you find the *precise* help that you need.

NATIONAL DOMESTIC VIOLENCE HOTLINES ✓

- ☐ 1-800 / 799 - SAFE
- ☐ 1-800 / 787 - 3224 (TDD)

INFORMATION & REFERRAL ✓

- ☐ Al-Anon
- ☐ Ala-teen
- ☐ Alcoholics Anonymous
- ☐ Catholic Charities
- ☐ County Bar Association
- ☐ County/Court Law Library
- ☐ County Medical Society
- ☐ Domestic Violence Coalition
- ☐ Legal Aid Society
- ☐ Mental Health Society
- ☐ Narcotics Anonymous
- ☐ Parents Without Partners
- ☐ Private Attorney Consultation
- ☐ Public Library
- ☐ Public Telephone Directory
- ☐ Salvation Army
- ☐ Spouse Abuse "Hot-Line"
- ☐ Telephone Info. Operator
- ☐ United Way
- ☐ YWCA / YMCA
- ☐ 800 Line Info. Operator

PUBLIC/COMMUNITY AFFAIRS DESK

☐ County Clerk's Office
☐ Co./St. Legislator's Office
☐ Criminal Court
☐ Dept. Of Social Services
☐ District Attorney's Office
☐ Family Court/Probation
☐ Federal Information Center
☐ Mental Health Clinic
☐ Police Department
☐ Public Hospital
☐ State Information Center
☐ Town/City Hall
☐ Victims Advocate's Office

SEARCHING FOR LISTINGS

Various services listed by non-profit organizations may go by *different* names depending on the sponsoring agency and the particular locale where such service is listed.

Examples: "Abuse," "Domestic Abuse," "Family Protection," "Family Services," "Victim's Assistance," "Crisis Intervention," etc.

Check the "Community Access" pages of your telephone directory for assistance.

AVAILABILITY OF SERVICES

Services offered by recognized national or regional organizations may vary from state to state and county to county. Always verify availability in your area with the local chapter.

MENTAL ILLNESS

Let's look at a different scenario. Your partner is not violent, not particularly abusive....just acting strange, different, out of character. Though he's not breaking any laws, his irrational behavior is causing you concern....maybe even a degree of fear for your safety or his.

It is *possible* that he is showing *signs* of "mental disability," *defined* generally to encompass "mental illness, mental retardation, developmental disability, alcoholism, substance dependence or chemical dependence." Such a condition could have a serious impact upon your relationship, your home life and your family.

This segment will offer suggestions on procedures which may be *available* for arranging for the *immediate* observation, care and treatment of persons who *may* be in need of such attention on a voluntary *or* involuntary basis.

Note that the specific requirements and protocols for your locale should be obtained from your legal counsel, police department or county mental health agency.

VOLUNTARY ADMISSION

Barring some traumatic or extraordinary impetus, the voluntary admission of an abusive or violent individual for psychiatric evaluation is a less than likely proposition.

INVOLUNTARY ADMISSION

If immediate inpatient care and treatment in a hospital is deemed *appropriate* by an examining physician, such admission *may* be obtained through application to such hospital by protocols established by the state or county mental health agency.

Police officers are normally expected to assist by taking such person into custody and transporting as required and directed by proper authority.

EMERGENCY ADMISSION

A person who is apparently mentally ill and conducting himself in a disorderly manner which is likely to result in serious harm to himself *may* be brought before the *court* upon issuance of a warrant for such purpose.

Police officers are ordinarily empowered and authorized to forcibly take such person into custody for purposes of examination or admission to an appropriate hospital or emergency facility.

Part 3 - C

REPRESENTATION

D epending upon *your* particular domestic situation, you may or may not require legal representation.

Issues such as difficulty in dealing with the "system," the possibility of counter-charges leveled against you, marital problems, custody battles, child and spousal support claims or other complicated legal matters where intimate knowledge of the law is required and negotiating acumen is helpful, call for the skills and services of a qualified attorney.

LEGAL ADVICE

If you are currently employed, you *may* be fortunate enough to have a prepaid legal plan as part of an employment benefit package.

Such plans generally cover routine legal matters such as consultations, preparation of wills, small claims cases, closing transactions, filing for bankruptcy and divorce.

If you think you *may* be covered with such a benefit, contact your personnel manager or employee benefits coordinator.

SELECTING AN ATTORNEY

Your attorney is expected to protect your *rights* and *financial* interests, keep you *informed*, *expedite* your case and charge you a *reasonable* fee.

In order to aid in the selection process and minimize dissatisfaction with your attorney, the following suggestions should be considered:

☐ Interview *several* attorneys before deciding which one you want to represent you.

☐ Ask if the initial *consultation* is free.

☐ Ask if they have *experience* in handling your type of case.

☐ Ascertain the *fee* structure (hourly, flat fee or contingency) and the *amount* of the retainer.

☐ Inquire as to the method of billing.

☐ Get an idea of their procedural strategy.

☐ Ask how they intend to keep you abreast of the progress of the case.

☐ Seek to develop a good and comfortable working relationship.

☐ Insist that they discuss *important* decisions with you first.

But keep in mind, your lawyer can "fire" you....that is, he can *withdraw* himself from your case if you do not *cooperate* with him or repeatedly *fail* to respect his judgment as it pertains to the handling of your particular case.

COMMONLY ASKED QUESTIONS

Chances are, there *will* be questions for your attorney. Make a *list* and include any unresolved issues.

Make *notes* and attempt to clarify areas which are not sufficiently *clear* to you.

■ SAFETY ISSUES

▶ Under what circumstances, if any, can I *demand* that my partner be *removed* from the premises?

▶ Can I petition the court to have licensed *firearms* removed from the residence?

▶ Can I request police assistance to help ensure my safety and that of my children by *escorting* me to a *shelter* or other safe haven?

▶ Can I request the police to *escort* me into my dwelling to *retrieve* clothing and personal belongings?

▶ May I expect the police to assist me in obtaining medical attention?

■ PRE-ARREST

▶ What specifically constitutes a "family offense" in the jurisdiction in which I reside?

▶ Is there a legal designation for "family offense victim" in my locality?

▶ Are there any family offenses or domestic situations for which my partner *must* be arrested?

▶ Can I request and receive a *copy* of any incident reports filed by the police officer?

▶ What are the penalties for knowingly filing a false report with the police or court?

▶ Must I wait until an incident occurs until I request an Order of Protection?

■ POST-ARREST

▶ Will I be *notified* if the *state* decides that it will not prosecute, will dismiss the charge or will enter into a plea agreement?

▶ In such event, what recourse, if any, do I have?

■ CHILD ISSUES

▶ Can I obtain temporary custody of my children?

▶ Am I entitled to temporary child support?

CROSS - REFERENCE

Various legal *issues* and related *questions* to discuss with your attorney are contained in other portions of this publication as follows:

X **Court Proceedings:** matters relating to the filing, processing and handling of family court proceedings are in Part 2-C.

X **Defense:** issues concerning the defense of self, others, premises, property and other situations are in Part 2-A.

X **Family:** legal matters relating to your children, dependents and marriage are in Part 2-B.

X **Protection Orders:** procedural and technical questions relating to obtaining a court-issued order of protection are in Part 3-A.

Chapter Four

HELP ARRIVES

- ❏ Part 4 - A   INVESTIGATION

- ❏ Part 4 - B   APPREHENSION

- ❏ Part 4 - C   PROSECUTION

This page intentionally left blank.

Part 4 - A

INVESTIGATION

Y our local police department is *empowered* and expected to assist you when you are *victimized* by another member of society, including a "loved one." Usually before any constructive action is taken, the assigned or responding officers will conduct an investigation to acquire as much preliminary *information* as possible.

CALLING THE POLICE

This section will help to answer the question: What should I expect from the investigative phase?

RELUCTANCE TO CALL

Some citizens fear the police. The presence of uniformed officers in their home can be an unsettling experience, regardless of the circumstances. The sight of guns, night sticks, handcuffs, mace and such paraphernalia can intimidate victims *already* subject to intimidation and deter them from pursuing an official investigation into their domestic upheaval.

USING AN INTERMEDIARY

At this point, outside assistance could come in handy to bridge the gap between fear and reassurance. While the police are in the *home*, a domestic violence *advisor* on the *phone*, acting in an intermediary capacity, could help alleviate the anxiety inherent with a police investigation. *If* such a service exists in your area, utilize it to its fullest advantage.

OFFENDER PRESENT

Officers responding to a domestic abuse incident are *expected* to:

1.   Restore *order.*

2.   Take control of any *weapons* used, threatened or accessible.

3.   Obtain *medical* assistance if requested/required.

4.   Ascertain all pertinent *facts* by interviewing all parties.

5.   Determine whether probable cause exists that any *offense* has been committed.

6.   Ascertain if an *Order of Protection* has been obtained by the victim.

7.   Check for any outstanding family offense *warrants.*

8.   Inform victim that domestic abuse *can* and often *does* escalate.

9.   Advise all parties that family violence is a *criminal* matter.

10.   Provide victim with the location of *shelters* and other *services* as appropriate.

11.   Arrange for transportation *if* circumstances warrant and where *permitted* by Departmental regulations.

12.   Provide Domestic Violence booklet or literature, if applicable.

13.   Give victim the complaint/file/case/report *number* for her *records* (or copy if appropriate).

14.   Remain at scene until either party removes personal belongings if one chooses to leave.

15.   If an *arrest* is made, emphasize to victim and defendant that criminal action is being initiated by the *state*, not the victim.

16.   Advise victim to notify police if offender *returns.*

ACCIDENTAL OR INTENTIONAL ?

There will be times when the officer will have to determine whether your injury was the result of an accident....as *he* says it was and as you *may* now also agree because he's threatened or intimidated you.... or the result of an act of *abuse.*

To accomplish this task, the officer must rely upon skills ranging from specialized training, the interpretation of body language and the application of deductive reasoning all the way down to experience, intuition and basic common sense. As the officer begins to "soak in" the scene, the investigative juices start to flow and a logical determination should emerge.

BUILDING A CASE

Cases must be built from the moment the 9-1-1 call is placed. For this reason, 9-1-1 tapes should be *saved* for evidentiary value.

To aid in the building of a solid case against the abuser, the **officers** should:

✚ Make note of *statements* (i.e., "He hit me with a frying pan," "He knocked me to the floor," etc.) and *observations* (i.e., "victim crying," "swollen left cheek," "black & blue on right arm," etc.).

✠ Recognize and record evidence and incriminating details of domestic activities which constitute or border on a *violation* of law (including photographing injuries sustained and property damaged during the altercation).

In furtherance of the goal to build a case and *substantiate* an allegation of abuse, the **victim** should:

✠ In the absence of official photographic evidence, take her *own* photos of visible injuries for future reference.

✠ Maintain a personal "evidence file" of such photographs, including any threatening letters, notes, answering machine tapes, voice mail or e-mail, as well as medical records, police reports, court records, etc.

✠ Keep a diary or chronological list of abusive or violent episodes occurring within the relationship.

OFFENDER *NOT* PRESENT

When the offender is not present, the officers should:

1. Obtain *medical* assistance as necessary.

2. Secure any *weapons* which may present a danger to anyone present.

3. Ascertain all pertinent *facts.*

4. Determine if probable cause exists that a *crime* has been committed or an existing Order of Protection has been *violated.*

5. Conduct a *search* of the immediate vicinity for the offender if there is *reason* to believe that such a search may be *fruitful.*

6.   Ascertain possible *destination* of offender.

7.   Check for outstanding family offense *warrants* via computerized, statewide registry.

8.   Remain at scene/residence until satisfied that a risk of recurrence has *subsided.*

9.   Comply with pertinent departmental guidelines and regulations.

10.   Record *each* investigation of an alleged case of domestic violence whether or not a crime was committed or an arrest was made.

11.   Prepare *all* necessary forms and reports.

12.   Refer "Family/Household" members to Family Court *or* Criminal Court - Summons Part.

13.   Refer persons not legally married but currently/formerly living together in a family-type relationship to Criminal Court - Summons Part.

14.   Refer case to appropriate detective/investigator for follow-up.

15.   Advise victim to notify police if offender *returns.*

PHOTO OP

In order to assist the police in an investigation, be *prepared* with the following:

1.   A current photograph of your *partner* to enable visual identification if he is being *sought* by the police or a process server.

2. A recent photo of your *children*, also for identification purposes, in the event of an *abduction* or *kidnapping* by your partner.

CHILDREN PRESENT

If children are present, the officers are *expected* to:

1. Determine if there are any children in the home who may be *victims* of abuse/neglect/maltreatment.

2. Initiate investigation into and *report* instances of suspected child abuse/neglect/maltreatment if situation does not present imminent danger to child under 18.

3. Activate emergency *removal* proceedings if child under 18 is in *imminent* danger.

4. Prepare "Report of Suspected Child Abuse or Maltreatment."

5. Notify the State Central Registry.

SPECIALIZATION

In this age of specialization, most medium to large size police agencies have adopted organizational techniques which allow for their personnel to devote all of their time and talent to a particular area of concern (i.e., Homicide Investigations, Juvenile Offenses, Traffic Enforcement, Narcotics Investigations, Sex Crimes, Street Crimes, etc.).

Ascertain if your local police department has a Domestic Violence Unit....a specially trained officer or group of officers who devote full time and attention to the needs of the victims of domestic violence. If so, stop in one day and get acquainted. Get his or her phone number and extension and keep it handy.

In order to enhance the investigative process, the following tasks, which should be assigned to the Domestic Violence Specialist, would be of *particular* value to the *victim*:

- Investigate reports of domestic *incidents* which cannot be initially *pursued* by patrol officers.

- Act as *primary* information and referral resource.

- Analyze data collected through complaint reports and field investigations to uncover *patterns* of abuse.

- Assist in the serving of Orders of Protection, as necessary.

- Initiate *proactive* measures to combat violence in the home by uncovering patterns of unlawful behavior.

- Keep victims *up-to-date* on progress of police investigation.

- Cooperate and coordinate with District Attorney's office in the prosecution effort.

ASSESSMENTS

Will he ever try to *kill* you? At some point you may need to determine just how *dangerous* your partner is.

Though *all* batterers are dangerous, *some* are more *likely* to kill than others. When a batterer is *enraged*, not only is the partner endangered, but also *any* person *perceived* to be in the way and expendable, such as children, family members, friends, neighbors, go-betweens, police and other persons performing intervention or conducting investigations. For this reason, assessments should be utilized to their fullest potential.

LEVEL OF CONCERN

Your partner *pushed* you once, but you forgave him. After he punched you, you were angry for a few days but he won you back with a dozen red roses.

That same week, he *swung* at you but you saw it coming and ducked. So now you're getting *worried*. Just how dangerous is this guy, you ask yourself. It's not an idle question.

If a hurricane was brewing in the ocean and you lived anywhere in its *potential* path, you'd want to know first, where it's heading....second, how fast it's approaching....and third, how strong it is. Based on that information, you'd either sit back and relax or you'd *plan* for possible disaster.

Think of your *partner* as a potential hurricane....whose strength, direction and velocity must be assessed in order for you to *survive*.

DEFINITION

Concerning itself with the violent, coercive or threatening *conduct* of the batterer....this is an *evaluating* process.... whereby the **victim** reflects upon the *purposes* of the batterer's acts in light of his *beliefs* and past *behavior*....and then considers the *risk* of danger....represented by the batterer's conduct.

DYNAMICS

The evaluation and gauging of *lethality*....the outer limits of potential *danger*....is a complex, continuing and imprecise process....*not* a tool for certainty of prediction.

PURPOSE

To help determine the appropriate level and extent of needed *intervention* and to enhance the strategic construction of safety plans in light of the determined risk, thereby averting injury or death.

GOAL

To identify those times and circumstances in which the batterer is *most likely* to attempt injurious or lethal assaults.

CRITICAL AREAS OF VALUE

Effective evaluations are of particular importance in assessing the following areas:

✓ Recidivism

✓ Separation Assault

✓ Homicide

BENEFITS

Lethality assessment *encourages* the *victim* to:

✓　Accept the *seriousness* of the situation.

✓　Make the proper decisions relating to *safety*.

✓   Obtain an Order of Protection.

✓   Cooperate in the prosecution phase.

✓   Seek community-based *assistance*.

BENEFICIARIES

Q. Who, in *addition* to the *victim*, benefits from the effective use of a lethality assessment?

A. All those with a professional obligation to *warn* a potential victim of danger, *protect* against the risk inherent in a violence-prone individual or *require* punishment and/or therapy for the batterer, such as:

▶ Law Enforcement Officers
▶ Prosecutors
▶ Judges
▶ Pre-Sentence Investigators
▶ Parole Boards
▶ Intake Personnel
▶ Intervention Professionals
▶ Victim's Advocates
▶ Health Care Workers
▶ Employee Personnel Departments
▶ School Administrators

WHO SHOULD ASSESS ?

With knowledge of the proper criteria, assessments can and should be made by police officers, criminal justice system personnel, victim advocates and abuse counselors as well as family and friends and the *victim* herself.

WHEN TO ASSESS

Assessments should begin at the time of the *first* crisis call, be *updated* periodically and *continue* throughout the legal proceedings until it is reasonably certain that the batterer is no longer a part of the victim's life.

Responding officers should conduct an assessment at *every* call....no matter how many times they return to the same household.

HOW TO ASSESS

Interviews of the partners should be conducted *separately* to encourage candor from the victim.

Assessments, especially third party interviews, should be conducted *cautiously* and with a degree of *confidentiality,* lest the batterer become enraged by having outsiders meddle in his "personal business."

Victims should be assisted in assessing the threat posed by their partners. The objective input and confirmation of suspicions may propel the victim to take necessary and evasive actions to avert a tragedy.

BLUEPRINTS

Changes in patterns of *conduct* can be *recognized.* An *escalated risk* of adverse legal, social or personal consequences assumed by the batterer in recent violent or coercive conduct can be *detected.*

Statements as to the irrevocable "ownership" of the victim and his commitment to inflict deadly harm if she seeks separation can be *investigated.*

RELIABILITY / ACCURACY / CERTAINTY

Generally, the less information available about a batterer, the less likely that the assessment will be *accurate.* Also, many *variables*....unknown or beyond the control of the assessor....may *intervene* to enhance or reduce the element of risk.

Be that as it may, acting too vigorously to *protect* the victim is *preferable*....ethically, socially and legally speaking....rather than failing to act, ignoring known risks or circumventing appropriate interventions.

"I'VE GOT MY RIGHTS!"

So says the indignant batterer. But doesn't everyone? Freedom from government intervention in general and the imposition of court-ordered controls in particular, cannot be taken lightly.

The civil rights of the *accused* abuser must be *balanced* intelligently against the interests of the abused partner and children....who have a *basic* human right to live in security and tranquility, free from fear, coercion, abuse and violence.

The assessment process is a valuable tool in reaching the desirable balance between his rights and her risk....between his behavior and her safety.

POTENTIAL TO KILL

The *greater* the number of indicators demonstrated, coupled with the *intensity* thereof, the *stronger* the likelihood of a life-threatening attack:

☐ **Threats of Homicide-Suicide:** the batterer who threatens to kill you, your children, your relatives and himself MUST be considered *extremely* dangerous.

☐ **Fantasies of Homicide-Suicide:** the batterer who so fantasizes may be subconsciously *planning* the act. Detailed planning, the availability of the means to activate a plan or prior attempts to act out the fantasy MUST be examined with *serious* implications.

☐ **Weapons:** the possession of, access to, or past use or threatened use of a weapon upon you, a loved one or himself *increases* the potential for a lethal assault.

☐ **Hostage Situation:** the mind-set of a batterer who resorts to taking a hostage is indicative of a person acting out of rage and/or desperation. Such a person is to be considered highly *volatile* and *dangerous.*

☐ **Severely Depressed:** the batterer who sees little or no hope for his situation in life may be a *prime* candidate for homicide-suicide.

☐ **Aberrant Behavior:** if for example, there is a history of or a threat of arson, the use of fire as a weapon against others must be considered a distinct possibility.

☐ **Indifference to Consequences:** a pronounced increase of personal risk-taking or actions suddenly taken without regard to their social or legal consequences should indicate a lack of constraint which may *escalate* to lethal assault without warning.

☐ **Separation Trauma:** the thought of losing his partner may cause great *despair;* the thought of life without you may trigger *uncontrollable* rage.

☐ **Right to Retaliate:** having made you the focal point of his life and/or being heavily dependent upon you, he feels rejected and "betrayed."

☐ **Right of Possession:** here, the batterer believes that he has a *fundamental* entitlement to assume *total* control of you *without* interference from *any* person, agency or governmental entity.

☐ **Repeat Customer:** the batterer who has generated *numerous* 9-1-1 calls presents an ever-increasing risk of displaying life-threatening behavior.

☐ **Accessibility:** the easier it is for the batterer to locate and connect with you, the easier it is to inflict a degree of harm that he deems "deserved," up to and including *murder.*

☐ **Opening The Closet:** if the batterer in a gay or lesbian relationship has been securely closeted and now is at risk of *exposure*, the loss of "invisibility" may create a sense of *desperation.*

☐ **Assessor's Intuition:** the experienced professional can often get a *feel* for what is going on in the home by evaluating the overall conditions and circumstances of the case (i.e., statements, history, body language, reports, etc.).

MOST RELIABLE INDICATOR

The best indicator of *future* violence is *past* violence. All previously battered women are at risk and need to be aware of and alert to that fact, as do those who work with battered women.

CAUTION

Because the making of assessments constitutes a subjective judgment and conclusions may vary among those involved, a victim who truly *believes* that her partner is *dangerous* should act and plan accordingly.

Although a victim may express only marginal concern over life-threatening behavior, all parties concerned must always be aware of and primed for *unexpected* eruptions of violence. Caution must be exercised at *all* times, including meetings, court appearances, child visitation, etc.

POSITIVE RESULTS

Victims should be advised of the results of the lethality assessment if it indicates that the abuser is *likely* to commit an act of life-threatening violence.

Officers should make note of such results and activate the procedures necessary to protect the victim and any children involved.

The victim should be urged to contact the local battered women's program to further assess lethality and develop a specific safety plan.

DANGERS OF INACCURACY

Inaccuracy which results in a *low* risk evaluation can present a sense of *false hope* to the victim. False hope can cause the victim to *relax* her guard. Lowering one's guard increases one's *vulnerability.* This of course is dangerous.

On the other hand, *needlessly* raising fears and escalating intervention can become counter-productive. A civil rights case might be made if preemptive intervention is imposed upon someone who is *carelessly* assessed as a high risk for homicide.

Ironically, barring *overt* signs to the contrary, homicide....the most lethal of acts....is also among the most *difficult* to statistically predict.

SAFETY PLANNING

Adequate safety planning should strive to accomplish the following:

✓ Facilitate escape

✓ Seek safe shelter

✓ Deny the abuser *access* to the victim

✓ Avert further abuse

✓ Obtain Order of Protection

✓ Access community support

✓ Prevent escalating violence

Part 4 - B

APPREHENSION

Y our relationship has now reached a *critical* point. Whether it is at your urging, as a result of police initiative or due to some other form of intervention or development beyond your control, your partner is about to be *arrested*.

ARREST BASICS

An "arrest" is essentially the taking of a person into physical *custody* by authority of law for the purpose of *charging* such person with a criminal offense. As such, apprehension is a serious business and does not occur without *probable cause.*

Arrests must be *lawful*....that is, rightful, legitimate, authorized by law....and capable of passing judicial scrutiny in a court of law.

PROBABLE CAUSE

This term refers to a combination of facts, viewed through the eyes of a police officer, which would lead a person of reasonable caution to believe that a crime is being or has been committed. The element of probable cause forms the *cornerstone* of a *lawful* arrest.

Note that the probable cause standard applied in family offense/domestic violence offenses is *no* different from the standard applied in other criminal offenses.

DUE PROCESS

Once the offender is *lawfully* arrested, the *legal* process begins and *due process* of law comes to life. This simply means that the offender is *guaranteed* protection of his *rights* by the Fifth, Sixth and Fourteenth Amendments to the U.S. Constitution.

AUTHORITY TO ARREST

A police officer may generally arrest for:

▶ Any **offense**....with reasonable cause to believe such person has committed such offense *in officer's presence.*

▶ A **petty offense**....with reasonable cause to believe committed *in officer's presence*....but only if committed or believed by officer to have been committed within officer's geographical area of employment....and....arrest is made in such county or adjoining county.

▶ A **crime**....with reasonable cause to believe such person committed such crime....in officer's presence *or* otherwise.

TOOLS OF ARREST

In addition to training and experience, police officers are lawfully "equipped" (with prescribed conditions and/or limitations) with the authority to serve and execute warrants, arrest violations, break and enter into premises, engage in "close pursuit" out of the county/state, conduct search and seizure and use necessary force in order to effect an arrest.

All of this service and expertise is just a phone call away. For you....except in a bona fide life-threatening emergency....to take the law into your own hands, would be foolish. Calling 9-1-1 is your safest bet.

BENEFITS OF ARREST

An arrest may help to accomplish the following:

1. Demonstrate to the victim, the offender and the community that domestic violence is a criminal act which will *not* be tolerated.

2. Demonstrate to the offender that there are legal *consequences* to his behavior.

3. Provide for court-mandated punishment and/or supervision, treatment or other community intervention.

4. Deter future criminal behavior.

5. Prevent further injury to the victim.

6. Open doors to support services for the victim.

HELP!

He's been arrested. He's in the "system." Now he *needs you!* It could be to bail him out or come up with bond money. It could be to get him an attorney or arrange legal counsel. It could be to do errands or visit him in jail. It could be to provide transportation upon his release or tend to other needs which arise during his incarceration.

Should you now help him squirm out of the situation that *he* caused at *your* expense? This is a judgment call that only you can make but it should be made wisely and preferably with experienced counsel to *guide* you.

Points to Consider:

1. The relationship itself
2. The offense charged
3. The potential for recurrence
4. The propensity for abuse
5. The potential for violence
6. The advice of counsel

For many victims, his time in the system is *your* time to think, to plan, to get help. Use this time to your best advantage, because he will *not* be in jail forever.

If you choose not to expedite his release from the court system, screen your telephone calls with the aid of an answering machine. Make yourself scarce. If he threatens you over the phone for "abandoning" him in his time of need, save the answering machine tapes for future evidence.

For some offenders, especially those new at exerting power and control in a relationship, this first-time brush with the criminal justice system *may* be a wake-up call, even without harsh penalties imposed by the court. This is not to imply that follow-up counseling for the abuser is not necessary or appropriate.

Needless to say, the more violent and repetitious the conduct, the more necessary and appropriate the court-mandated punishment and treatment.

VICTIM'S PERSPECTIVE

Witnessing an arrest is not a pretty sight, especially if the arrestee is your spouse or the father of your children. Though you have experienced considerable stress and trauma already, be *prepared* for more but temper the added anxiety by considering the following:

1. Depending upon your personal feelings for the offender.... positive, negative, neutral....and the intensity of these

feelings, your stress level and guilt-o-meter will surely be affected.

2. When the offender is informed of his impending arrest, he may be cooperative, uncooperative or beg for you to withdraw your complaint.

3. For this reason, the offender must be informed by the arresting officer that criminal action is being initiated by the state and not the victim.

4. When an arrest is imminent, send the children to another room. There is no need for them to observe the procedure.

5. Police procedure requires that persons placed under arrest be restrained with handcuffs. Some departments may require defendants to be rear-cuffed for added security. As previously stated, it's not a pleasant sight.

6. Until the defendant is securely restrained, the *possibility* exists for a *dangerous* episode of resistance and physical confrontation.

7. Keep in mind that police officers may lawfully use physical force which they reasonably believe is necessary to effect the arrest, prevent an escape, defend themselves or defend others present.

8. Officers may lawfully use deadly physical force when confronted with deadly physical force to defend themselves or others or to effect an arrest or prevent an escape in cases involving certain felonies.

9. Because the arrest is a legal process wherein the defendant must now answer to a crime in a court of law, he is now a "client" of the criminal justice system.

10. Once the offender is arrested, your pity, tears, regrets, sorrow and second thoughts, may have emotional impact, but no legal bearing on the processing of the defendant.

Due to the nature of the police action taking place in your home....with its inherent anxiety and the emotional strain on all involved....coupled with the explicit potential for serious injury....it is usually advisable to *minimize* your presence (i.e., remain in another room) until the offender has been safely *removed* from the premises.

VICTIM'S INPUT

A full and complete statement should be taken from the victim. This opportunity gives her a "*voice*" in the matter. It should *also* prevent the offender from thinking that he was arrested for arbitrary reasons *unrelated* to the victim. If that were the case, it would serve to exacerbate the level of animosity and aggression upon his release.

DISCRETIONARY ARRESTS

When dealing with criminal offenses relating to domestic violence, the current legislative trend is to *limit* the amount of discretion available to police officers handling such cases. Hence, the enactment of legislation in some jurisdictions which *requires* that police "shall arrest....and shall not attempt to reconcile the parties or mediate...." in specified family offense situations.

In those instances when discretion is available, the following factors should be utilized to *gauge* the *appropriateness* of an arrest:

1. Victim's condition
2. Partner's demeanor
3. History of past incidents
4. Likelihood of imminent danger

MANDATORY ARRESTS

It would be beneficial for the victim or prospective victim to ascertain in *advance* of a domestic incident, what the mandatory arrest policy is for the jurisdiction in which she resides.

POST-ARREST PROCEDURES

Being the complainant/victim, you are a *participant* in the proceeding. You therefore have a vested interest in the outcome of such proceeding. As the case snakes its way through the corridors of justice, you have a right to know where things stand.

From the time of arrest, you must ask: "what happens next, where are they taking him, will he be kept overnight, when will he see the judge, what should I do now?"

To assist and enlighten you along these lines, seek the assistance of a victim's advocate whenever availble. They can "stay the course" with you until the case is finalized. The arresting officer, assisting officer, booking officer and desk officer can provide you with information relative to the immediate issues at hand but cannot provide legal advice, nor walk you through the system as the victim's advocate can.

In any event, ask questions of whoever is available at the time. Get more names and make notes. Clarify any confusing points or fill in any gaps with the district attorney's office if necessary.

Depending upon the offense charged and various factors relating to his history and personal circumstances, the offender *may* be (in chronological order):

■ **RELEASED....**prior to court arraignment
(eligible for "station house bail," issued Desk Appearance Ticket or official notice to appear or discharged for lack of adequate criteria to constitute a valid arrest)

■ **RELEASED**....upon court arraignment
(eligible for bail, released on personal recognizance or dismissed by judge on legal or technical grounds)

■ **HELD**....upon court arraignment
(ineligible for bail or release on personal recognizance, outstanding warrant pending, violation of terms of probation/parole, at judge's discretion or required by statute)

■ **RELEASED**....upon motion or hearing prior to trial
(dismissed on legal or technical grounds or pending trial date)

■ **RELEASED**....at pre-trial hearing
(per conditions set by court)

■ **RELEASED**....after acquittal at trial

■ **RELEASED**....after serving a sentence of incarceration

The variables in each case are numerous and no two cases are alike. For this reason you need the advice and counsel available to you from support and advocacy groups. Avail yourself!

PLEASED VS. DISPLEASED

If you believe that you have *cause* to be displeased with the police intervention/investigation, by all means speak up. If on the other hand you are *satisfied* with the overall handling of your case, speak up also. Your local police personnel appreciate an occasional pat on the back.

TERMINOLOGY

The following terms are defined for your *general* information. Keep in mind that *precise* definitions will vary among the various jurisdictions.

RE: UNLAWFUL ACTS

CRIME

"a misdemeanor or a felony"

FELONY

"an offense for which a sentence to a term of imprisonment in excess of one year may be imposed"

MISDEMEANOR

"an offense, other than a 'traffic infraction,' for which a sentence to a term of imprisonment in excess of 15 days may be imposed, but for which a sentence to a term of imprisonment in excess of one year cannot be imposed"

OFFENSE

"conduct for which a sentence to a term of imprisonment or to a fine is provided by any law of this state...."

VIOLATION

"an offense, other than a 'traffic infraction,' for which a sentence to a term of imprisonment in excess of 15 days cannot be imposed"

RE: POST- ARREST

ARRAIGNMENT

"the occasion upon which a defendant against whom an accusatory instrument has been filed appears before the court in which criminal action is pending for the purpose of having such court acquire and exercise control over his person with respect to such accusatory instrument and of setting the course of further proceedings in the action"

DESK APPEARANCE TICKET

"a written notice issued and subscribed by a police officer or other public servant authorized by state law or local law....directing a designated person to appear in a designated local criminal court at a designated future time in connection with his alleged commission of a designated offense"

INDICTMENT

"a written accusation by a grand jury....filed with a superior court, which charges one or more defendants with the commission of one or more offenses, at least one of which is a crime, and which serves as a basis for prosecution thereof"

RELEASE ON OWN RECOGNIZANCE (R.O.R.)

"a court releases a principal on his own recognizance when, having acquired control over his person, it permits him to be at liberty during the pendency of the criminal action or proceeding involved upon condition that he will appear thereat whenever his attendance may be required and will at all times render himself amenable to the orders and processes of the court"

SUBPOENA

"a process by which a court directs the person to whom it is addressed to attend and appear as a witness in a designated action or proceeding in such court, on a designated date and any recessed or adjourned date of the action or proceeding"

RE: BAIL

BAIL

"cash bail or a bail bond"

FIX BAIL

"a court fixes bail when, having acquired control over the person or a principal, it designates a sum of money and stipulates that, if bail in such amount is posed on behalf of the principal and approved, it will permit him to be at liberty during the pendency of the criminal action or proceeding involved"

POST BAIL

"to deposit bail in the amount and form fixed by the court, with the court or with some authorized public servant or agency"

Part 4 - C

PROSECUTION

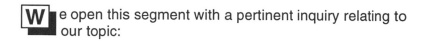

W e open this segment with a pertinent inquiry relating to our topic:

Q. What is the "system" which we refer to throughout this publication?

A. "System" can be short for "criminal justice *system.*" The CJS consists *primarily* of the police, prosecutors and judges and includes their resources and support staff. On a *secondary* level, the CJS includes the public defenders, probation, parole and correctional departments.

In an abstract sense, the "system" encompasses all persons, agencies and entities which are expected to *intercede* on behalf of the victims of domestic violence and *protect* them from further abuse.

In order for there to be a *successful* prosecution, three entities of government must join forces:

POLICE - who must *investigate* the complaint and *arrest* the offender.

PROSECUTOR - who must *evaluate* the allegation and *present* the case before the appropriate court.

JUDGE - who must *supervise* the court proceedings as they apply to the *charges* against the defendant and sentence or otherwise dispose of the case in accordance with prevailing law and procedure.

THOUGHTS & THEORIES

We are now interested in knowing how these three components of the criminal justice system can work together to better serve the victims of domestic violence.

We have examined the role of the police in Part 3-B (Intervention). This section will explore the work of the prosecutors and judges as they help to make the "system" work.

Keep in mind, if one link in the chain of cooperation and teamwork breaks, the entire protective and remedial process stumbles and fails.

NEED FOR PROSECUTION

A clear, unequivocal message *must* be sent to the batterer that the victim, the "system" and the public will *not* tolerate domestic violence. What is perceived to be indifference on the part of *any* branch of the criminal justice system constitutes tacit approval of abuse and consequently *encourages* recidivism.

Exposing the batterer and taking him "out of the closet" can.... with the exception of the most recalcitrant offender....have a *deterrent* effect on recidivism.

WHY PROSECUTE ?

The criminal justice system must be guided by the *nature* of the abusive *act* and *not* the relationship between the abuser and the abused. Whatever the relationship may be, an act of domestic violence is *no* less a crime than an act of violence between complete strangers.

If justice is "blind," why does the "system" peek to see if the complainant and defendant are related? Definitions of crimes do not change because the two share an apartment. Assault is assault, rape is rape, murder is murder. The Penal Law does not differentiate between victim and offender in order to lessen the charge or the punishment. Being a housemate or lover does not provide immunity from prosecution or "Brownie points" at the sentencing phase upon conviction.

The husband or boyfriend who beats his partner should receive no more consideration from the "system" than the mugger who attacks an old lady on her way to the grocery store. One, is no less a criminal act than the other.

The fact that the domestic abuser is a nice guy at work or a friendly neighbor on the block or a member in good standing at a local civic association make him no less a criminal law violator than the town bully who likes to start fights when he doesn't get his way.

WHO PROSECUTES THE ABUSER ?

The "people" of the state, through the State Attorney or District Attorney's office, press charges against those who are alleged to have violated laws governing human behavior; *not* the victim of such behavior.

The "prosecutor" is a district attorney or any other public servant who represents the *people* in a criminal action.

ACCOUNTABILITY IS ESSENTIAL

Very little progress will occur unless the offender is held legally and socially *accountable* for his actions. Accountability is essential or the entire process is *meaningless.*

In order to foster accountability for the offender's behavior, the victim should be interviewed whenever a request is made to drop a minor charge against the partner. Dropping charges in rubber-stamp fashion *defeats* the ends of justice and *fuels* the cycle of abuse.

Also, little ground will be gained until the offender is given the *help* necessary to change *his* ways. Since *he* is the problem, mediation and couples counseling are *not* effective strategies for dealing with violence.

VICTIM AS COMPLAINANT

"He didn't mean it." "He won't do it again." "I got him angry." "It's really my fault." "I blew things out of proportion." Does it sound familiar?

You might as well just say you're not a victim.

WHO'S IN CHARGE HERE ?

Except for headline-making incidents, tradition has dictated that the criminal justice system should comply with the wishes of the victim....wishes that vacillated between "Just get him out of here" to "Put him in jail and throw away the key!"

With "regular" or non-domestic offenses, the "system" does not abdicate decision-making to the victim. So too with domestic violence, the victim should not be able to call the shots and in effect, manipulate the proceedings.

The overall public interest must take precedence because the abuser is violating society's laws, putting a strain on the criminal justice system and a drain on the limited tax dollar.

The more domestic abuse offenders there are in society who continue to flaunt the law, the more society will suffer directly and indirectly, now and in the future.

"KEEP ME OUT OF IT"

Hesitancy or reluctance to cooperate in the prosecution effort is grounded in several factors:

▶ Commitment to the marriage vows

▶ Desire to keep the family together

▶ Belief that the partner will change

▶ Sense of guilt, shame or embarrassment

▶ Financial dependency upon the abuser

▶ Perception of having nowhere to go

▶ Third party interference

▶ Fear of retaliation

Note that these "reasons" are very similar if not identical to the "reasons" for remaining in the abusive relationship.

"LET'S CALL THE WHOLE THING OFF"

The dynamics of a relationship often cause an *ambivalence* towards the arrest, prosecution and punishment of a spouse or lover.

Basic affection yet fear of reprisal, sense of loyalty yet need for relief, family ties and financial considerations, conflicting emotions and conflicting advice....all work at cross-purposes to tug at your feelings and your sense of propriety.

Though you want the abuse and violence to stop and for your partner to receive help, the sight of his being handcuffed, taken away and locked up is often too much to bear....especially since he is now *pleading* for you to intervene, *promising* never to hit you again.

"LET'S GO FOR IT !"

Just as more victims are willing to seek *protection* through the court by way of an Order of Protection, an increasing number of victims are willing to cooperate with *prosecution* efforts in the courts.

Word of mouth and support groups are helping victims discover that this can be a battle worth fighting.

Accusations however, must *not* be filed frivolously. Charges made purely out of anger or revenge are bound to *backfire.* Filing a false report of an incident can be either a misdemeanor or felony, depending upon the circumstances, likewise for the offense of perjury.

GETTING YOUR DUE   ✓

☐ Solicit information and assistance from the Crime Victim's Compensation Board, if appropriate.

☐ Inquire how and when your *property* (if entered into evidence) can be returned.

☐ Request restitution or reparation in cases where injury, damage or economic loss is sustained, as deemed appropriate.

☐ If restitution or reparation has been ordered by the court, make *note* of the terms and conditions of payment by the defendant.

KEEPING TRACK   ☞

☐ Make every effort to keep abreast of the progress of the court case.

☐ Inquire as to where the defendant will be incarcerated and for how long.

☐ Inquire as to what procedures, if any, are in place to be notified of the defendant's release, transfer or escape from prison.

☐ Obtain the name and phone number of the defendant's probation/parole officer.

☐ Notify the District Attorney's office of any change of address/telephone number.

MISCELLANEOUS REMINDERS ✓

☐ Remember to dress appropriately for judicial hearings and court appearances.

☐ Report instances of intimidation or harassment by the defendant, someone acting on his behalf or by any unknown person/s.

PROSECUTOR'S ROLE

The prosecutor is the vital connecting link between the police officer and the judge. His basic function is to represent the victim (and the "people") and put forth a sound case before the court.

As an integral part of the criminal justice system, prosecutors must collaborate with their colleagues and contemporaries in getting out the message that domestic violence will not be tolerated in our society.

OPERATING POLICY

A public policy of "no reversal" on the part of the District Attorney's office in handling domestic violence cases may help counter the effect of outside interference and may help dissuade persons from attempting to thwart a prosecution, once locked in "forward gear."

Other administrative policies of a *progressive* nature include:

- Placing a high(er) priority on domestic violence cases.

- Avoiding the practice of dismissing misdemeanor or violation cases.

- Refraining from diluting the *seriousness* of some charges by resorting to the use of pre-trial intervention programs in lieu of criminal sanctions and appropriate follow-up programs.

- Assigning one prosecutor for the duration of the case.

- Implementing a specialization program within the prosecutor's office.

- Establishing a liaison officer to work with the other branches of the criminal justice system.

- Re-examining plea bargaining policies.

- Re-evaluating administrative and operating procedures and gauging their *effectiveness.*

EXPECTATIONS

What should you expect the prosecutor to do or hope to accomplish regarding the prosecution phase?

◘ Seek and maintain your cooperation and confidence.

◘ Charge all possible violations of law committed within the statute of limitations.

◘ Charge any and all misdemeanors along with felonies.

◘ Develop a particular *strategy* for presentation of the case.

◘ Strive to build a solid case, achieve a conviction, ensure a just sentence and survive an appeal.

◘ Utilize the preliminary hearing for its maximum benefit to corroborate and protect the case.

◘ Record and preserve your testimony.

◘ Allow you to experience testifying similar to that of the actual trial.

◘ Recreate the *emotion* of the offense.

◘ Understand the *psyche* of the defendant.

◘ Develop *power* and *control* issues in the relationship.

◘ Allege a "continuous course of conduct" if permissible.

◘ Seek rulings on the admissibility of prior conduct and prior convictions.

- Argue for admissibility of medical records or prior assault convictions in order to prove motive, opportunity, intent, identity or the absence of mistake or accident

- Present *all* available and lawful evidence.

- Seek to *exclude* inadmissible defense evidence.

DON'T EXPECT MIRACLES

One must remain *realistic*. Some District Attorney's offices are understaffed and operate with less than adequate resources. Many offices, especially in the large cities, are inundated with huge case loads. Human error, to varying degrees, is inevitable.

In some cases, there may be little or no corroboration. Witnesses may become reluctant, change their version of the facts, leave the jurisdiction or be of less than perfect character.

For these reasons, *you* should attempt to keep on top of the case as it progresses (or flounders) through the halls of justice. Conferring with the Victim's Advocate will be very helpful at this point.

DEALING WITH VICTIMS

Victims should be *encouraged* to go forward with their cases. But for a variety of reasons....some reasonable, some not....the prosecutor will often encounter the reluctant, uncooperative complainant.

Fortunately, there is a growing tendency on the part of many prosecutors to file and pursue criminal charges against abusers *without* the victim's collaboration. This "zero tolerance" policy.... especially vital in serious cases....requires an operating strategy in order to be effective.

INTERVIEWING THE VICTIM

In an effort to lay the ground rules, establish a good rapport and develop a positive working relationship with the victim, the prosecutor should:

- Advise the victim that she can choose whether or not to continue the relationship, but she can not choose whether or not he will be prosecuted.

- Explain that the District Attorney's office is *not* attempting to *persecute* the defendant.

- Inform the victim that she is *not* responsible for the violence.

- Explain to the victim that the *defendant* must take responsibility for his anger, stress, substance abuse, etc.

- Explain further that he cannot change on his *own.*

- Evaluate the impact of threats, intimidation, economic support issues, children, length of relationship, history of abuse, low self-esteem, drug or alcohol use.

- Understand that the victim may not be *ready* to make the *necessary* changes in order to protect herself and her children.

- Warn the victim how *kind* and *loving* her partner may be while the case is *pending.*

- Advise the victim that she has access to whatever support services are available throughout the proceeding.

- Discuss the various sentencing options which may be available.

■ Emphasize the *strong* possibility that the defendant may be *released;* then allow the victim to make her decision based on her *knowledge* of the defendant's past behavior.

VICTIM'S STATEMENTS

It is of *paramount* importance that the victim's statements be accurate, truthful and consistent. The prosecutor should get the victim committed to a *credible* version of the facts as *soon* as possible....including a high degree of *detail* in all statements....in order to make recantation or denial difficult.

Audiotaping the statements of victims and witnesses should be utilized to help achieve this goal. Videotaping the victim's injuries will create a permanent record for the court.

Prior *inconsistent* statements must be dealt with by the prosecutor by means of a *strategy* developed for such purpose.

THE UNCOOPERATIVE VICTIM

When dealing with a reluctant victim, the prosecutor should:

1. Treat the victim carefully and without exerting undue pressure.

2. At the *risk* of having the case *dismissed,* decide whether to keep such victim from testifying.

3. Develop her *motive* (based upon fear) to lie and protect her mate.

4. Utilize any and all relevant hearsay statements where legally admissible.

5. Present any and all pertinent medical records and physical evidence.

Hesitancy on the part of the victim to actively participate, cooperate and assist in the prosecution effort may be overcome or significantly reduced by providing or helping to arrange for:

✓ **Protection;** by the processing of an Order of Protection through the court.

✓ **Information;** by explaining the court process which is about to take place.

✓ **Support;** by referring the victim to available counseling and intervention services.

✓ **Encouragement;** by building morale, especially in those who have no faith in the "system."

THE CHILD WITNESS

Since children are often present when violence erupts, the prosecutor must address certain issues and questions, such as:

▶ Did the child make a statement to police at the scene?

▶ Will the benefits of intervention *outweigh* the emotional trauma of testifying?

▶ Is the *risk* ot abuse greater if the child testifies against the abusive parent? (It usually is!)

▶ Can the child be provided with advocacy and support, via court order, after testifying?

In addition to his other duties and responsibilities, the prosecutor must....based upon legal guidelines and established precedent....*assess* the competency and credibility of the child and develop a *rapport* with such witness before the trial.

PROSECUTOR'S CHECKLIST

■ **WITNESSES:**
- ☐ The Victim
- ☐ Children
- ☐ Family Member
- ☐ Household Member
- ☐ Neighbor
- ☐ Landlord
- ☐ Police Officers
- ☐ Paramedics
- ☐ Personal Physician
- ☐ Nurse
- ☐ E.R. Admit. Clerk
- ☐ Attending Doctor
- ☐ E.R. Nurse

■ **EVIDENCE:**
- ☐ 9-1-1 Tapes
- ☐ Statement Copies
- ☐ Victim Photos
- ☐ Scene Photos
- ☐ Clothing
- ☐ Blood Samples
- ☐ Semen Samples
- ☐ Sketches/Diagrams
- ☐ Weapons
- ☐ Police Reports
- ☐ Medical Records
- ☐ Phone Records
- ☐ Protection Application

JUDGE'S ROLE

In the abstract sense, judges play a critical role in shaping the community's overall response to domestic violence.

As interpreters of the law, judges play a pivotal role in how the accused will be dealt with (in terms of leniency, punishment, mandates, etc.) once convicted.

ON THE BENCH

Judges can determine the kind of attention paid to family violence cases by exerting their extraordinary influence and authority as system advocates and helping to *educate* the public as to the *criminal* nature of domestic violence.

Knowledgeable family law judges can effectively:

✓ Propose legislative changes and improvements.

✓ Advocate the need for increased resources to address various aspects of the domestic violence problem.

✓ Require feedback from law enforcement agencies if too few cases are coming before the court.

✓ Encourage improvements in policy, procedure, data collection and record keeping among the various agencies which deal with domestic violence cases.

JUDICIAL POLICY RE: VICTIMS

When focusing upon the *victim*, the presiding judge should:

✓ Issue Orders of Protection as necessary to *protect* the victim, family members and all other persons who may be endangered by the violent or threatening nature of the offender's behavior.

✓ Eliminate any hint of gender *bias* in the courtroom.

✓ Address the victim's fear of *retaliation.*

✓ Consider *safety* issues when determining the release of the offender on bail or personal recognizance.

EXPANDED ROLE

The effectiveness of judges is further examined in Part 5 in segments titled Discretion, Incarceration and Rehabilitation.

JURORS AS SPOILERS

Months of investigation, preparation, presentation and determination can be *undone* in a matter of hours or minutes by a jury. How can this happen?

1. A domestic violence *survivor* may be *less* sympathetic to the victim if such survivor left *her* relationship *without* outside intervention.

2. A professional woman may view the *chronic* victim *negatively* since *she* would *leave* any man who hit *her.*

3. A macho-oriented male may interpret the modern approach to handling domestic violence as a *threat* to "tradition" and *his* manhood.

4. A male may identify with the *defendant* in that he views women as the weaker or inferior gender.

To help prevent seating or developing a potentially weak juror, the prosecutor should:

✓ Phrase questions so as to place the potential juror in the victim's shoes in order to *uncover attitudes* on spousal abuse.

✓ Educate and inform potential jurors by asking tough questions and drawing them into discussion if reluctance becomes apparent.

✓ Probe for bias; the potential juror may be hesitant to join with the prosecutor to "interfere" when the victim chooses not to pursue the matter.

✓ Focus jurors on the *state* as prosecutor, *not* the victim.

✓ Prepare jurors for an *uncooperative* victim, if necessary.

Chapter Five

TIME FOR CLOSURE

❏ Part 5 - A   DISCRETION

❏ Part 5 - B   INCARCERATION

❏ Part 5 - C   REHABILITATION

This page intentionally left blank.

Part 5 - A

DISCRETION

The concept of discretion is a tool which allows the presiding judge to utilize his discretionary powers to benefit *both* victim and abuser. Needless to say, discretion must be used with caution and prudence.

COURT-ORDERED INTERVENTION

Once the interests of the victim have been met as to support, counseling, protection, etc., the court should focus primarily on the *offender*....the ultimate goal being to *stop* the violence.

The arrest routine without any sort of constructive intervention (i.e., commensurate punishment, professional counseling and mandatory therapy) may be nothing more than a mere inconvenience for the abuser....a temporary interruption from his normal way of handling things at home.

INTERVENTION PROGRAMS

Court-ordered requirements to attend a violence intervention program presents a special and valuable opportunity for the defendant to:

1. Keep his abusive/violent behavior in check.

2. Keep from going to prison.

3. Keep from getting a criminal record.

4. Keep from losing his job.

5. Keep his family intact.

SETTING BAIL

   The arrest-release revolving door must be significantly slowed for the sake of the victim, her children and any other person residing in the household....as well as any innocent person who might otherwise be subjected to the aggression of the abuser.

   Where there is *room* for discretion, the *sensible* setting of bail can act as an aid in achieving and preserving victim cooperation. Bail arguments (For vs. Against) should focus upon:

▶ the *seriousness* of the offense

▶ any use of a *weapon*

▶ any outstanding *warrants*

▶ *prior* arrest history

▶ *likelihood* of serious injury

▶ any *death* threats

▶ any *substance* abuse

▶ the *history* of abuse/violence

▶ any *roots* in the community

▶ possibility of *fleeing* jurisdiction

   As a prosecution tool, where lawfully permissible, keeping a defendant in custody can often expedite a plea. Allowing release from custody once responsibility is *acknowledged* and long-term treatment is *agreed to* can be an effective prosecution strategy in some cases.

As a safeguard to better insure against the defendant's reneging on his agreement, *probation* must be incorporated into any such agreement.

PROBATION

Probation provides the offender with an opportunity to avoid incarceration. But this should *not* be looked upon as a "gift." Certain specific conditions *must* be met, such as:

✓ Refraining from further abusive behavior.

✓ Compliance with an Order of Protection.

✓ Participation in a counseling program.

These provisions benefit the victim. But in order for the concept to work, probation must be *monitored* to assure *compliance.* If a violation occurs, probation must be *revoked,* whereupon *additional* sanctions and/or requirements are incurred.

Orders of Protection which were issued as a condition of pre-trial release should be *extended* through the probationary period as a source of *added* security for the victim.

Probation personnel should abide by clearly articulated de-partmental policies and procedures and be trained and prepared to recognize and respond to domestic violence matters in every area of their job (i.e., intake, investigation, supervision, etc.).

When the court weighs the *feasibility* of probation, it should consider if any of the following factors are relevant:

◼ Any weapons used?

◼ Any physical injuries sustained?

■ Any hospitalization required?

■ Any permanent injuries sustained?

■ Any subsequent contact during the prosecution phase?

■ Any prior assaults in private?

■ Any prior assaults in public?

■ Any prior injuries or hospitalization?

■ Any assaults (past/present) on child or family member?

■ Any sexual assaults (past/present) on child/family?

■ Any threats made in connection with prosecution?

■ Any history of violence including attempted homicide, suicide or both?

■ Any prior Orders of Protection issued or renewed?

■ Any revelations of homicidal-suicidal thoughts, fantasies or intentions?

■ Any other pertinent past or present acts or statements made by defendant?

Part 5 - B

INCARCERATION

W ith a few notable exceptions (i.e., some homeless, destitute or elderly persons who enjoy a *better* quality of life *in* prison than on the *street*) no one wants to be incarcerated. That includes your abusive partner.

Even if he's been in before, going back now because he "merely expressed" himself in his own home, is a deep blow to his pride and his manhood.

Should you feel sorry? Probably not. Should you feel concerned? Probably so.

But he must understand that *you* didn't put him in jail, the *judge* did....for something unlawful that *he* did.

COURT POLICY RE: DEFENDANT

When focusing upon the *defendant*, the trial judge should send a clear message that such defendant shall be held *accountable* for his actions and that the court *refuses* to tolerate unlawful behavior in public or in private.

Whenever possible, the judge should *maximize* all avenues, sanctions and options available to the court for the purpose of *ending* the violence including mandatory, supervised, abuser counseling and education programs as *part of* sentencing or as a *condition of* probation.

JUDICIAL DETERRENT

Offenders who are not dissuaded by a police officer's authority to *arrest,* are more likely to be dissuaded by a judge's authority to *incarcerate*. This is especially true for those offenders who have been arrested numerous times before *without* consequence.

AS AUTHORITY FIGURE

A stern judge can be the offender's worst headache. An overly lenient judge can be the victim's worst nightmare. But a fair and reasonable judge can work within the system to bring about the desired results: an *end* to the violence.

Such judge can and should:

✓ Deliver clear, authoritative judicial messages to the offender.

✓ Influence the future behavior of *some* offenders through verbal admonishments and warnings.

✓ Order *mandatory* participation in treatment programs for offenders not amenable to such reprimand.

✓ Address the issues of drug and alcohol abuse, if applicable.

✓ Administer criminal sanctions where appropriate.

SENTENCING

The sentencing phase should generally be geared toward holding the offender *accountable*, *ending* the abusive behavior and meeting the *needs* of the victim and family members. Lenient sentences tend to *undermine* the seriousness of the defendant's actions.

Sentencing should ultimately address the *fundamental* issues: power, control and violence.

■ Fines may punish the *victim* if there is a support order in effect or other ongoing economic aspect to the relationship. The offender may consider a modest fine "just the price of doing business."

■ Work release programs should be utilized where appropriate to allow for ongoing *financial* support of the family.

■ Incarceration should be evaluated with an eye on the *victim's* needs and preferences (unless such wishes would result in overly lenient penalties) as well as the *seriousness* of the offense.

■ Weekend incarceration should be considered in less serious cases in order that the offender may continue to work and support the family.

■ The duration and frequency of long-term counseling should jibe with the circumstances and severity of the offense.

■ Probation with a *suspended* jail or prison term can be effective in dissuading further criminal behavior for some defendants.

■ Restitution should be considered as part of a sentencing arrangement as a means for holding the offender responsible for expenses incurred by the victim as a direct or indirect result of such offender's behavior (i.e., medical fees, lost wages, damaged property, etc.)

THE COURT & PUNISHMENT

Of the various components of the criminal justice system, only the *courts* can inflict punishment upon a citizen of the state for a violation of the law or of a court mandate.

POWER OF ARREST

The act of being physically arrested, restrained, interrogated, fingerprinted, photographed and placed in a detention cell with one or more of society's miscreants can have a sobering effect on most people....except perhaps those for whom the scenario is second nature or for those so hardened by its frequency, that the procedure has lost its sting.

Unfortunately, as for deterrent value, an arrest in and of itself is usually insufficient to prevent future violence.

COURT POLICY

A victim who gains the strength and courage to become *intolerant* of domestic abuse will be discouraged and frustrated if she encounters a court system which is *tolerant* of abuse. Intolerance must be pervasive and universal. A "rupture" at any point along the pipeline to justice will cause the best of plans and intentions to fail. Such failure is a "win" for violence.

Incarceration, even if brief, is often the best means at the court's disposal to *impress* upon the offender that violations will *not* be tolerated.

DEFENSE POSTURE

In the *ideal* world, the defense attorney, especially a privately retained defense counselor, might....to demonstrate good faith to the court and deter a recurrence of violence....require the abuser to *stop* his behavior and attend counseling *before* agreeing to represent him. This bold but *unrealistic* scenario would surely help end recidivism.

But in the *real* world of the adversarial criminal justice system, defense attorneys, especially public defenders who cannot pick and choose their clients, must *defend* these abusive and violent defendants in a court of law, *regardless* of the frequency and severity of the offense.

WHO'S THE VICTIM HERE ?

Often times, the defense attorney will conjure up a dazzling depiction of victimization upon the *abuser*....he, because of his unfortunate background and life experiences, is the "real victim" in the case.

This strategy encourages the abuser to *resist* therapy and deflects needed attention from the legitimate victim: the *abused* partner.

THE INADEQUACY OF PUNISHMENT

We now know that battering can *never* be justified or excused. Punishing the batterer may be fundamentally appropriate as a form of societal retribution but it usually accomplishes *little* more than that.

Often the offender will leave prison as an angry and embittered individual who has been "scorned" by his partner and the "system." Anyone who believes that he will return home "a new person" is in for a sad surprise.

This is not to imply that incarceration is without merit. Sending the offender off to prison is both appropriate and necessary in cases involving:

✓ serious violence.

✓ a long, continuous pattern of abuse.

✓ unsuccessful results with alternatives to incarceration.

✓ significant threat of continued harm if the offender is not incarcerated.

THE CONTRITION REPETITION

Many abusers are very contrite *after* the violence and even *after* an arrest for such violence. Apologies and regrets served on a tray of tears may seem sincere. They may in fact *be* sincere.

But promises made without professional counseling and back-up support are often a road to temporary forgiveness but not permanent peace.

Part 5 - C

REHABILITATION

As we near the end of our discussion on domestic violence, a parting word on the *need* for rehabilitation of the *abuser* is in order.

Though the focus of this publication has been on the safety and well-being of the *victim* and her family, without an abuser there would be *no* victim. Stated more succinctly: no abuser....no victim! Is this not a goal of universal importance?

A ROSE IS A ROSE IS A ROSE

The unemployed batterer who finds employment is *still* a batterer. The alcoholic batterer who joins an A.A. program is *still* a batterer. The incarcerated batterer who is punished by the court is *still* a batterer. The impoverished batterer who wins the lottery and satisfies all his material needs is *still* a batterer.

Get the picture? Whether employed or out of work....substance-free or addicted....wealthy or poor....famous or infamous, without a specific treatment program for this individual to address his *behavior*, he will *remain* a batterer.

SOCIETY'S DILEMMA

Solving Mary Smith's problem by getting John Smith out of the house does not solve society's problem. The act of *leaving* solves only *half* of the domestic violence problem in this particular case. Although the batterer has no one to batter for the moment, he is *still* a batterer.

Soon there will be a Jane Smith.... a new victim for John Smith to fall in "love" with. Then, sure as the sun rises in the East each morning, the cycle will begin all over again....the threats, the fear, the abuse, the battering, the 9-1-1 calls, the Orders of Protection, the arrests, ad nauseam.

Violence will continue and escalate, dragging more victims down into the pit of pain and despair....introducing the next generation to the tragedy of becoming or creating victims themselves.

MEN ARE LIKE RODENTS ?

Just as laboratory rats can be *trained* by rewarding *good* behavior and withdrawing reward or punishing for *bad* behavior, human beings can respond to the scientific concept of "behavior modification" as well.

Relatively *petty* relationship violations such as *chronic* lateness or unacceptably *rude* phone conversation can be addressed by informing the "violator" that a *continuation* will result in your leaving without him or hanging up on him. After thus *asserting* yourself, your job is to follow through.

Equally important in your goal to modify behavior and encourage needed improvements is the task of praising *good* behavior and showing appreciation where appropriate.

Such do-it-yourself therapy however, may apply solely to the *early* stages of relationship problems. Domestic *violence* cases will require the experienced intervention of a *professional* therapist.

REHABILITATION FOR THE ABUSER

Except for the expressly violent defendant who requires incarceration and therapy, the "psycho-educational" format of a violence intervention program should provide an **end** to the abuse by:

■ Teaching defendants to take *responsibility* for their actions.

■ Helping them *understand* their abusive, controlling behavior and its *impact* on themselves and others.

■ Developing self-esteem and respect for others.

As "punishment" for their actions, defendants should be required to pay for their sessions. If however, they are truly indigent, the opportunity to help them should not be forsaken for lack of personal funds.

Successful completion of the program is imperative, lest the defendant sleep through the course or fake his way through and forfeit the opportunity to turn his life around for the better.

DENIAL

Most abusers are in denial....much as the alcoholic or drug dependent person who *refuses* to concede that they have a serious problem.

If they make any admissions, they *minimize* their abusive tendencies *and* the effects upon their partner and children. After all, they "don't beat for nothing."

Violence is a *learned* behavior which can be *unlearned.* Unfortunately, it is difficult to get the typical abuser into treatment *voluntarily* because of this tendency to deny and because of their unwillingness to accept responsibility for their behavior.

Though voluntary participation and a sincere desire to change is the *ideal,* court-ordered counseling is the next best alternative. Ordering counseling in lieu of incarceration can be a powerful incentive for the offender. Since the primary goal of counseling is to *stop* the violence, everyone stands to gain if such effort is successful.

WHAT WORKS ?

Punishment *alone* is not enough to *correct* a battering syndrome, since it does not *change* the offender....it only *postpones* the next assault. A diversified *treatment* program without punishment will generally do *more* good than punishment applied without treatment.

Rather than merely *punish* the offender, the criminal justice system must strive to *change* the offender....that is to say his ways, his behavior, his thinking, his attitude.

To be significantly effective, treatment must bring about an *immediate* halt to the violence and a *long-term change* in the abuser's behavior. How? Through a combination of psychological and educational techniques....and because no two situations are alike....custom-made or specially adapted strategies or variations to accomodate the abuser's behavorial mode.

If this can be accomplished....through professional counseling and competent therapy....*everyone* will benefit.

Mandatory counseling *coupled with* probation for misdemeanor and first-time offenses should be encouraged because of their inherent benefits.

The fact that counseling *may* resolve the underlying problem in the relationship and that *no* criminal record and *no* jail time accrues to the defendant, *encourages* the victim to *cooperate* in the prosecutorial process.

Conversely, the establishing or adding to a criminal record and shipping the partner off to jail *dissuades* the victim from cooperating and testifying in a criminal proceeding. Sadly, many ripe cases "die on the vine" for lack of satisfactory evidence when the victim will not testify.

MEDIATION & COUNSELING

The mediation of disputes resulting in or precipitated by abusive behavior can be a step backwards in that it can allow a *manipulative* partner to gain *control* of the process and steer the blame *away* from himself. If however, it can bring about *counseling* for the *abuser*, it may ultimately be worthwhile.

Mediation is *not* appropriate however, for domestic *violence* offenders since it would require the victim to participate in the sentence and relies on the mutual goodwill and sense of fairness of both parties....one of which has *already* exhibited manipulation and total control over the other.

Family therapy and couples' counseling may address family problems, marital relationships, conflict resolution and communication dysfunction. But such programs view battering as a symptom of a problem in the family or in the relationship and do *not* focus on the violence committed by the sole offender.

This philosophy is harmful in that it can reinforce the batterer's habit of *denying* responsibility for his behavior, *minimizing* the problem and *transferring* blame onto his partner. This sequence helps the offender to effectively *facilitate* his resistance to change.

Though these valid issues and problem areas may need attention, the violence must *stop first.* Consequently, family and couples' counseling is appropriate only if *both* partners seek it voluntarily and the offender has already succeeded in *ending* his violent behavior.

WILL IT HELP ?

For some offenders, battering represents a complex, deeply ingrained behavior pattern that is *not* easily altered. Conventional group counseling and educational programs may be *inadequate* for these cases.

As with the treatment of complex disorders such as alcoholism and substance abuse, *varied* approaches may be necessary for such individuals.

One method to circumvent the problem is to refer offenders to professional counselors for an *evaluation* to gauge the potential for success in using available programs.

ROAD TO RECOVERY

Abusers need to keep in mind that they have the *potential* to be violent. When, where, how and why is determined by them....in conjunction with the particular circumstances which *incite* their aggressive behavior.

Negative and destructive attitudes must be altered *before* behavior can be *permanently* changed. With an emphasis on the importance of *respecting* women, counseling must attempt to develop a more flexible male identity and more realistic *attitudes* and *expectations* towards women.

Sexist beliefs which are not addressed may prolong psychological control long after the physical abuse has subsided.

The cornerstone of a solid cure includes:

✔ acceptance of *responsibility* for abusive behavior.

✔ identification of other forms of *controlling* behavior.

✔ creation of *alternative* ways of expression.

MAKING A DIFFERENCE

Abusers must learn how to behave differently; how to react to problems and setbacks differently; how to treat their mates and children differently.

THE DROP-OUT

Generally speaking, the longer a person remains motivated *and* the longer he remains in the program, the *greater* the chances of success.

Lack of internal motivation, *coupled* with limited legal consequences accounts for the high drop-out rate among abusers, many of whom drop out within a month....some as soon as a reconciliation occurs.

Why bother? they ask. What's the motivation? They got their "property" back, and besides, *they* don't need any help.

Unfortunately, restoration of the status quo outweighs the desire to change. If it becomes clear that reconciliation is not possible, dropping out is almost inevitable.

If the batterer drops out of a counseling or therapy program, this indicates that he is not committed to changing his behavior.

His dropping out is *not* your fault. The onus to change abusive behavior is on the *abuser*.

This page intentionally left blank.

Chapter Six

TURNING POINT

❏ Part 6 - A   RECONCILIATION

❏ Part 6 - B   TERMINATION

❏ Part 6 - C   RECUPERATION

This page intentionally left blank.

Part 6 - A
RECONCILIATION

I t is said that only a good marriage in trouble can be saved and that a bad marriage in trouble can only get worse. Accepting that premise....while acknowledging that there are exceptions to every rule....we will examine the conciliation process and its relevance to your situation.

QUALIFYING ASPECTS

Contrition and remorse are the salve of forgiveness and renewal. Pledges and promises *may* bring about a rebirth of the relationship.

Common sense dictates that this avenue is *not* open to everyone. If however, your abusive relationship has *not* reached the violent stage....is essentially verbal and emotional in nature....and *both* parties wish to salvage the union, the conciliation process *may* be of value (See "Salvageable Relationships" before proceeding).

WHAT IS REQUIRED FROM THE ABUSER ?

Both parties must participate in the conciliation process but the *primary* obligation to succeed falls upon the abuser. Since he brought about the problem, nothing will change without his all-out effort, such as:

1. A *sincere* desire to *change.*

2. An *acknowledgment* that his behavior is *unacceptable.*

3. A willingness to accept *responsibility* for his *behavior.*

4. Enrollment in a series of counseling sessions to address his propensity to *control* his partner.

5. Progressing to an advanced therapy program to address *anger* management, if necessary.

6. Addressing his substance abuse problems, if any.

WHAT IS REQUIRED FROM THE VICTIM ?

As the victim, you play a secondary but nonetheless major role in achieving a satisfactory resolution to your domestic situation. The following duties are assigned to you:

1. Monitoring the *attendance* record of the abuser.

2. Gauging his level of *determination* to succeed with the program.

3. Measuring the *progress* or absence thereof.

4. Counseling for yourself to *cope* with any eventuality.

5. A back-up *plan* if the abuser fails to succeed in his efforts at meaningful change.

6. Patience. Fortitude. Resolve.

FOLLOW-UP REQUIRED

If, after the abuser successfully completes his counseling or therapy program, the relationship requires supplemental assistance to address relatively minor but nevertheless irritating issues, a joint marriage or couple's counseling effort may be productive.

FAMILY COURT SERVICES

Ascertain if the family court in your community sponsors a reconciliation program for marriages in trouble. A program of this nature, conducted under the auspices of an official branch of the criminal justice system, can provide a degree of formality, structure and purpose....and would enable the victim to become familiar with the operation of family court including its jurisdiction, powers and services.

Hopefully, the abuser, once taken under the watchful eye of the court, will be coaxed into a compliant mode of behavior.

PRACTICAL ASPECTS

A judge or social worker *cannot* rejuvenate your relationship....especially one that has become *violent.* As for a *salvageable* relationship, both you *and* your mate must strengthen it from within by working on, improving and striving not to neglect the following:

- **COMMITMENT to each other;** a bona fide commitment should enable *both* partners to overcome obstacles.

- **COMMUNICATE with each other;** already critically important, go a step further and create an atmosphere where there is freedom to talk about *difficult* emotions.

- **MAINTAIN OPENNESS;** frank, honest discussion helps to keep the *channels* of communication open.

- **CONSIDER PARTNER'S NEEDS;** ascertain your partner's *emotional* needs and *personal* desires....compare his with yours discovering similarities and differences.

◻ **SET PRIORITIES;** establish *reasonable* goals but prioritize, based on *realistic* factors within your personal, marital, economic and family circumstances.

◻ **RESOLVE CONFLICTS;** attempt to resolve conflicts within the relationship and the family unit *before* they escalate into major confrontations.

◻ **ACCEPT DIFFERENCES;** acknowledge that *everyone* is different and *no one* is perfect.

◻ **LEARN TO APOLOGIZE;** a *sincere* apology can help relieve the pressure of a stressful marital spat.

◻ **LEARN TO FORGIVE;** this can help to balance the equation and *stabilize* the parties in a dispute.

◻ **BE REALISTIC;** visualize the *ideal* relationship in reasonably *attainable* terms; include desirable features worth striving for rather than merely hoping for.

◻ **LAUGHTER and GOOD WILL;** laughing with each other, at each other, or at one's self can aid significantly in reducing the stress meter.

◻ **SPIRITUAL AWARENESS;** look within and reach back to your spiritual foundations or seek to develop a guiding relationship with your personal spiritual entity.

◻ **SEXUAL INTIMACY and LOVEMAKING;** with a goal of *mutual* satisfaction, this pleasurable endeavor can provide an opportunity to demonstrate care and concern for your partner.

BATTLE TECHNIQUES

Before doing "battle" with your partner, review the following anger management and control techniques:

Schedule Your Discussions:

◉ Set aside *specific* times to discuss that which is troubling your relationship.

◉ Meet *regularly* to get a grip on the problem(s).

Control The Setting:

◉ Since an audience can create a theatrical atmosphere, choose the *location* of your discussions carefully.

◉ Avoid personal and controversial issues and heated discussions in front of *others*, especially children.

Focus On The Issue:

◉ Avoid rehashing *old* and basically resolved issues or resurrecting *past* admissions of wrongdoing.

◉ Avoid veering off into *petty* annoyances and *unsubstantiated* accusations.

Focus On Yourselves:

◉ Avoid dragging *others* in to critique or referee your dispute.

◉ Avoid using *other* "model" couples as a frame of reference.

Listen First:

- Hear each other out without *needless* interruption.

- Avoid a running *commentary* or the constant interjection of *sarcasm.*

Keep Your Calm:

- *Resist* the urge to shout or get physical.

- Vocal and visible anger adds *fuel* to the fire of discontent and becomes *counter-productive.*

Avoid Misunderstandings:

- Attempt to *clarify* ambiguous or conflicting statements.

- Avoid making *assumptions* based on vague or insufficient information.

Refine Your Style:

- Discuss rather than debate.

- Avoid *monopolizing* the discussion.

Terminate As Necessary:

- Take a *break* if either partner is getting emotionally charged up.

- Reschedule the discussion if *tempers* begin to erupt.

Stay On Track:

- Evaluate your degree of progress *or* impasse.

- Seek professional counseling *if* deemed appropriate.

STUMBLING BLOCKS

Suppose that your partner in a non-violent relationship is *unwilling* or not ready to go for help or seek solutions? What can you do?

1. Attend counseling session *alone*; this will help *you* and demonstrate your *seriousness* to others.

2. Avoid holding a grudge or resorting to spiteful, vindictive behavior; this will only *exacerbate* the situation.

3. Avail yourself of support from family and friends; this will provide an ear to listen, a shoulder to cry on and a mind to share some wisdom and experience.

4. Abandon your surroundings; this will provide a temporary but refreshing change of scenery and a chance to boost your morale.

5. Halt a heavy duty debate in mid-stream; this *may* avert a violent outburst and give your partner a chance to calm down a bit.

6. Alter the mood; try some soft music, mild exercise, a short walk or other soothing diversion.

GETTING "UPSET"

A normally compatible and congenial partner can, at various times and for various reasons, get "upset" about something you've just said. Many times it's not the message per se....it's the delivery, the implication or the ramifications of the statement.

Perhaps you've just bought something that he believes will adversely affect the monthly budget. Maybe you've done something else that he honestly believes was ill-advised.

Whatever the case may be, defend your point of view and argue *without* resorting to an *attack* upon your partner's character, intelligence or values.

Rather than press the "hot buttons," try to inject some *levity* into the discussion. Humor and affection can help to keep a debate from getting out of control.

Keep in mind that *good* news should be shared between partners as well as bad. An interesting article from the newspaper, an amusing story from work or an especially funny joke can help keep the communication process civilized, productive and enjoyable.

Part 6 - B

TERMINATION

The stay-leave question is one of the most crucial (and difficult) issues which you will face in your relationship. Hopes, desires and reality will collide in a head-on crash of emotions.

At this stage of your education about domestic violence, you should be aware that abusive men often *escalate* their aggression to recapture the partner who has "escaped." You should also know that the need for medical attention often *increases* during the separation sequence because the abuser's self-imposed authority has been seriously challenged and his overall control has been substantially threatened.

Unfortunately, the act of leaving can cause you to be tainted as a quitter....or it may result in your being seen as causing or compounding your own problems. If you *leave* the children, you may be seen as an insensitive, unfit mother. If you *take* the children, you may be accused of depriving them of their father and his support....or....of being an ungrateful wife.

Yet another consideration: if the *children* are also being *abused*, the court or child welfare agency *may* issue an "emergency removal order" of the children from *both* parents because the battered mother is not able to protect her children from her partner.

This potential double whammy could be all the more reason to remove yourself and your children from the abusive environment masquerading as a home.

It's always easy to blame the victim. But guess what? It doesn't matter. Your personal safety and that of your children is of *paramount* importance.

For these reasons....and there are others....leaving an abusive home is a *major* decision. Once your abusive partner knows that you have left or suspects that you intend to leave, you are in *added* danger.

But *sometimes*....because of the reasons discussed in this segment....staying a bit longer, can be the *lesser* of two *evils.*

ECONOMICS

Unfortunately, out of economic *necessity*, abuse is the "price" some women pay in order to *maintain* their standard of living, *especially* when there are *children* to raise.

Though the *quality* of life is *lacking*, the alternative (leaving) results in *further* disruption of family life (especially for the children) and severe economic *hardship.*

The "price" paid must be *weighed* against each victim's reading of her "tolerance meter" (i.e., # 1 being relatively *mild* abuse such as of a verbal nature to # 10 being outright physical abuse of a *violent* nature).

STAYING

There can be many reasons why the victim stays. Reasons generally focus upon physical danger, personal difficulty and extraneous factors often beyond her control. One, some or all of the following reasons can apply to any given relationship:

PRACTICALITY

Fear - fear of leaving can be *greater* than the fear of staying. Fear of unknown consequences, further injury and even death can *deter* many victims from leaving.

Futility - previous attempts at seeking help from the Criminal Justice System or various intervention agencies have not yielded the desired results. If anything, the abuse has substantially intensified.

Economics - financial dependency upon the male partner is often a *primary* reason for remaining, *especially* for women with children and without marketable skills.

OBLIGATION

Children - may be held "hostage" by the abuser if victim attempts to leave. Also, the fear of raising children *alone* can be a strong *deterrent* to leaving.

Guilt - the abuser will often get "sick" and "need" his partner to *stay*. On top of that, family admonitions can sway one's sense of obligation to remain.

EMOTIONAL

Love - most women hate the *behavior* but love the *partner.*

Promises Of Reform - this "music to the ears" usually turns a sour note.

False Perception - a belief that once the abuser realizes just how *serious* the abuse is becoming, he will (sort of automatically) *stop*. After all, he's really not that bad a guy. Right? Wrong!

PERSONAL

Religious Beliefs - often reinforce *submission* to the partner and *commitment* to the marriage.

Lack Of Self-Esteem - the victim may come to *believe* that she somehow *deserves* the abuse.

Conditioning - many women are *passive* by nature and/or upbringing and therefore *dependent* upon men. Women who accept responsibility for the condition of their relationship may *hesitate* to leave thereby *admitting* failure.

Ignorance - the *absence* of knowledge as to the availability of legal remedies and support services can help to keep the victim stuck in her rut.

SOCIETAL

Social Attitudes - the more people who believe marital violence is *acceptable*, the easier it is for the *cycle* to *continue.*

Social Stigma - people who consider children from "broken" homes as *inferior*, help perpetuate the stigma attached to families that *separate* to escape a dangerous and violent home life.

ALWAYS THE VICTIM ?

How much can you tolerate? Infrequent displays of what outwardly appears to be affection....the tenderness reminiscent of the pre-marital courtship....is not worth the price of frequent abuse.

Victimization doesn't depend on whether dinner is served on time or whether you have satisfactorily performed your chores or whether you displeased your partner in some other way.

His behavior is *his* doing and it will *not* change unless and until someone can *convince* him....or a judge can *order* him to get professional help. If neither of these motivating factors materialize into momentum, then *you* must get the help you *need* to leave.

Insomuch as you *fail* or *refuse* to get needed *help,* you are perpetuating your own abusive lifestyle.

LOVE OR ADDICTION ?

He's so possessive, so domineering, so demanding, so abusive! Are you *really* "in love" with the brute?

Instead of love in a genuine and mature sense, you may.... because of a *dependence* upon him and a need to *escape* from yourself....be addicted to your partner. Such addiction, by nature of most addictions, is but a *quick fix* which aids the *symptoms* but not the *cause* of your problem.

Breaking your addiction however, will require *withdrawal.*

LOVE, LIKE OR LUST ?

If you can't honestly say that you love him, do you at *least* like him....or do you simply lust for him? Strong sexual attraction....in the *absence* of any emotional foundation or ties....can *distort* your reasoning process and blur your vision of impending *danger*.

Some women who have endured a lack of male companion-ship *may* be so anxious for attention and intimacy that they throw intuition and caution to the wind in their quest for personal and emotional fulfillment.

Relationships based *solely* upon sex are doomed to fail. Once the "love-making" gets routine....and with the absence of genuine affection....there is *nothing* left to fall back on, allowing abusive behavior to waltz right into the "love nest."

JUST WHAT IS LOVE ANYWAY ?

Love is hard to *precisely* define or explain because it is a feeling, an emotion....both simple *and* complex in nature. What then *do* we know about the mystery and magic of love?

Not a game or contest of wills, love is an emotional energy and capacity tapped from an inner reservoir of affection for others.

Love is *more* than fondness and admiration. Love *exceeds* sentiment and concern. Love goes *beyond* passion and intimacy.

Love is a freely-offered, unconditional commitment of mind and spirit which provides peace, strength and inner joy. It is one of life's truly rewarding experiences which gives meaning and purpose to one's existence.

Can there be *more* to love....this "emotional feeling"....this word which is thrown about so casually? There *is* more.

Love is precious and priceless....timeless and endless. Love is warmth and sensitivity....comfort and satisfaction. Love is fulfillment and contentment....excitement and enjoyment.

Love is dedication and devotion....mutuality and togetherness. Love is unselfish sharing and sacrifice.... the pleasure of giving and pleasing.

Yet love comes with duty and responsibility. Love requires honesty and sincerity....trust and reliance. Love requires loyalty and fidelity....equality and exclusivity. Love requires mutual respect and openness....toleration and compromise.

For some however, love can be rare, infrequent or non-existent. It can be a cause for celebration when it's attained or a cause for sorrow when it's lost.

Now, for a most vital question: does this discourse on love match what *your* partner feels *and* exhibits towards *you?* If it is one-sided and *not* mutual, it is an airplane without wings....it will *not* fly!

WHAT WILL IT TAKE ?

If a poisonous snake was slithering under your bed, you'd run out of the house fast. If a grizzly bear was at the table eating your porridge, you'd get out real quick.

If a time bomb was ticking under your couch, you'd exit the premises pronto. If your house was contaminated with an infectious disease, you'd evacuate immediately.

If a tornado was heading your way, you'd run in the opposite direction. What do these scenarios have to do with *you?* Give it some thought. Do you see *your* spouse or domestic partner in any of these *analogies?*

Wild animals, inanimate objects and forces of nature do not have the capability to *love* the victims of their wrath.

Some victims of terror and violence *must* leave in order to protect their *lives* and preserve their *sanity*. If you can not analyze the import of these examples on your own, get professional help.

"But it's *my* house" you say. Then *he* must leave....voluntarily or by extraneous persuasion, police intervention or a court order.

Keep in mind that if your partner doesn't love you, you're pushing boulders uphill....the higher you get them, the stronger the force against you when they begin to roll back down upon you.

DECISION TIME !

How much *can* you take? How much *will* you take? These questions must ultimately be answered.

No two partners are alike. No two situations are alike. Each victim must *evaluate* her personal and family circumstances (i.e., number and ages of children, physical and emotional health, finances and economic resources, job skills and employment history, access to auto or other transportation, support and assistance services and other personal considerations). Then decide:

1. Should I leave?

2. When will I leave?

3. Where will I go?

4. Who can I confide in?

5. What will I take?

6. How will I function after leaving?

LEAVING

Persons *unfamiliar* with the scope and dimensions of domestic violence often have a *simplistic* retort when commenting on the plight of the victim: "Why doesn't she just leave?"....or...."She must like getting hit." But the victims, their family members, counselors and students of domestic violence know better.

The act of leaving is not simply a matter of walking out the door. Leaving in and of itself does *not* assure long-term safety and tranquility. Successful departure is best accomplished when it is planned in advance, strategic by design and backed with legal and community protection.

Except in the case of an *emergency* exit, this prescription for success must not be attempted hastily. Because of the *stress* associated with an abusive relationship, many women make a number of *attempts* before being able to accomplish their *safe* departure.

TEMPORARY VS. PERMANENT

Leaving is sometimes a temporary maneuver....providing an opportunity to gauge the reaction of the abuser and/or explore the world outside the home. Such interludes can and should be a *learning* experience for the victim and a wake-up call for the abuser.

In the *absence* of concrete change for the *better,* the leaving process must become *permanent* as long as it does not further jeopardize the victim's safety.

The need for police intervention and prosecution follow-up *increases* in proportion to the increased level of *danger* to the victim.

REASONS FOR LEAVING

Reasons for leaving are many and varied. The primary and most common among them include:

Serious Injury - resulting from a severe battering incident (most women seek *help* soon after a serious assault).

Child Abuse - initiated or escalated by partner (many women will tolerate their own abuse but *not* that of their children).

Awakening - an internal awakening to the *reality* of the situation (things will *never* get better and she just *can't* take it anymore).

Awareness - the discovery of outside *assistance* not known before (the new found availability of resources designed to aid the victim can open new doors).

IT'S SELDOM EASY

Utilizing psychological barriers, the abuser may threaten to do one or more of the following:

■ Withhold support

■ Cause other financial hardship

■ Seek custody of the children

■ Harm victim or another person

■ Interfere with employment

■ Spread false rumors

■ Turn others against victim

FINANCES

Finances are the fuel to fight inertia. The best of intentions will leave you idle without the necessary economic resources. Without the required funds, the road to recovery is virtually closed to you.

What avenues can you take to circumvent these roadblocks?

◼ Liquidate dispensable assets.

◼ Borrow from any legitimate source.

◼ Request temporary support through the court.

◼ Seek support award in protection order.

◼ Solicit assistance through Dept. Of Social Services.

◼ Pursue job training programs.

◼ Explore employment opportunities wherever possible.

HOW BEST ACCOMPLISHED

◉ When *planned* properly. (See "Survival Tips").

◉ When initially *aided* by a *trusted* companion.

◉ When receiving follow-up *support* from a social service program. (See "Resources")

EFFECT UPON ABUSER

Ironically, leaving or attempting to leave (which usually *seems* like the ideal *solution*) often dramatically *increases* the risk of *danger* to the victim.

The abuser often feels that he has *lost control* and will go to great lengths to *regain* it. In many cases this may begin with tracking, stalking and harassing; then lead to serious physical assault. When the abuser believes he's licked, he may resort to *murder* in order to have the "*final say*" in the matter.

Knowing this, many women subject to battle fatigue become immobilized by fear and suffer in silence....unable or unwilling to leave the relationship.

EFFECT UPON CHILDREN

The most dangerous time for the child is when the union is dissolving. The more committed the father is to continuing his dominance and control, the more dangerous it is for the child.

Since the child is an extension of the mother.... who "dares" to seek her independence.... hurting the child is a tactical way to exert dominance and control of the mother.

In addition to physical harm, children run an increased chance of being abducted by a father who has been "cut off" from the family unit. Abduction usually occurs as a means of terrorizing the mother and retaliating for challenging his authority and interrupting the status quo.

You must be aware of and alert to the fact that custodial interference can occur at any time after the separation or divorce.

REALITY CHECK ✓

Economically speaking, studies and statistics reflect a *bleak* outlook for the newly "emancipated" woman with children. For many such women without adequate alimony, child support, wages and/or other substantial and reliable income, a poverty-level existence is not uncommon, especially in the early stages of separation or divorce.

Various forms of *discrimination* which may manifest themselves in the housing and job market (though technically illegal) will also *hinder* the victim from blending into mainstream society and establishing a peaceful family life (i.e., racial, ethnic, economic, gender, family and social status, etc.).

SURVIVAL TIPS

☐ Prepare a *detailed* safety plan *beforehand.*

☐ Ascertain pertinent laws and available resources from the local domestic violence center, preferably *before* a crisis.

☐ Select a *trusted* person to confide in and keep *informed* of your on-going domestic situation.

☐ Keep records, make notes or maintain a diary.

☐ Keep a spare set of keys, change of clothing, important papers, prescriptions and money with a reliable friend, neighbor or family member.

☐ Call the *police* if you or anyone in the home is in *danger.*

☐ Notify local police of any *recent* act of violence which has not yet been reported.

☐ Obtain or renew Order of Protection through Family Court, as necessary.

☐ Arrange a distress signal with a *reliable* neighbor (i.e., porch light on = call police!)

☐ Seek medical/hospital treatment if needed and request documentation.

☐ Do not antagonize your spouse by *challenging* his "*authority*" in threatening to leave.

☐ Plan the *safest time* to get away.

☐ Instruct your *children* where to go in the event of a problem.

☐ Assure them that you will seek assistance and protection for *them* and *yourself.*

☐ Carry phone numbers of persons who can assist you including a domestic violence shelter.

☐ Take any *evidence* of physical abuse with you (i.e., torn clothing, doctor bills, photos of bruises or injuries, etc.)

☐ Avail yourself of whatever victim's *services* may be necessary and available in your area.

☐ In *extreme* cases, it may be *necessary* to move out of state and change identity, even after the divorce is final.

CELLULAR PHONES

If *financially* feasible, cellular phones can provide a sense of security when out of the house or if the residence line is de-activated. There are however, some drawbacks:

1. There may be no automatic re-dial if cut off.

2. They do not transmit caller location.

3. Routing procedures for 9-1-1 response may vary in different localities.

To *minimize* delay, you should give the following information to the emergency operator:

1. Your current *location* (as precisely as possible).

2. Your *direction* of travel (if in motion).

3. Any *landmarks* (just passed or approaching).

4. Your vehicle *description* (type, color, make, model, plate number).

5. Description of vehicle *following* you (including its driver).

6. Any other *relevant* information (including any known weapons involved).

LONG-TERM NEEDS

Check the boxes which may apply to you and your particular situation upon or soon after divorce or separation....things to do, things to acquire or things to contemplate.

Use the line following each item to jot down a pertinent name, phone number or other relevant information on that particular topic.

■ HOUSING
- ☐ Address, notify change of _____
- ☐ Furniture Storage; in/out _____
- ☐ Lease, sign new/break old _____
- ☐ Permanent Housing _____
- ☐ Phone Number, change _____
- ☐ Security Deposit, make/recover _____
- ☐ Utilities; on/off _____

■ HEALTH COVERAGE
- ☐ Medicaid (State) _____
- ☐ Medicare (Federal) _____
- ☐ Plan Coverage _____

■ LEGAL MATTERS
- ☐ Alimony, Permanent _____
- ☐ Annulment Proceedings _____
- ☐ Child Support Proceedings _____
- ☐ Custody, Permanent _____
- ☐ Deed, change/transfer _____
- ☐ Divorce Proceedings _____
- ☐ Guardianship _____
- ☐ Spousal Support _____
- ☐ Visitation _____
- ☐ Will/Codicil _____

■ FINANCIAL
- ☐ Assets, liquidate _____
- ☐ Bank Account, open/close _____
- ☐ Credit Card, apply for _____
- ☐ Debt Consolidation _____
- ☐ Financial Statement, prepare _____
- ☐ Investments, make/transfer _____
- ☐ Joint Accounts, cancel _____
- ☐ Loan, Personal; apply for _____
- ☐ Tax Preparation; refund/pay _____

■ PERSONAL
- ☐ Adult Ed. Course; register _____
- ☐ Auto Insurance; acquire/modify _____
- ☐ Auto Registration, change _____
- ☐ Auto Title, transfer _____
- ☐ Beneficiary, change _____
- ☐ Career Enhancement _____
- ☐ Life Insurance; acquire/modify _____
- ☐ Resumé, prepare/update _____
- ☐ Social Club/Group, join _____

AFTER LEAVING

1. Secure your home as finances permit (i.e., change locks, install metal doors, smoke detectors, outdoor lighting, security system).

2. Obtain or renew Order of Protection, as necessary.

3. Request neighbors to call police if they see your former partner on or about the premises.

4. Inform your children's caretakers (school, day care, baby sitter) of the names of persons who are permitted to pick them up.

5. Join a support group in your area.

VISITATION

Visitation *can be* a source of heightened stress and anxiety for all concerned. It may be misused to gain access to the mother, it can compromise the mother's safety and it can create an adverse emotional impact on the child. There are however, various ways to lessen the potential for problems.

AGREEMENTS

Visitation agreements should be *modified* if visitation privileges:

- Are being *abused* in any manner.
- Are being used as a bargaining tactic to *coerce* a reconciliation.
- Are being used to manipulate or coax the victim into *dropping* a criminal complaint.
- Provide an opportunity to jeopardize the mother and/or child's *safety.*

SHORT FUSE

Visitation can provide the batterer with an opportunity to discuss a reconciliation. The "discussion" often leads to a debate. The debate frequently leads to an argument. An argument then brings about an assault.

At this stage in the confrontation, it doesn't take long to get from point "A" to point "B" and so on. The cycle of violence is quickly re-ignited.

To add fuel to the fire, the sight of his former partner.... obviously on her way out for the evening....dressed in a sporty new outfit, new hair style and make-up....can trigger a violent reaction.

You want to assert yourself....to demonstrate that you are now your own person. But is it wise to rub it in his face *too* hastily or too prematurely....*before* he's had a chance to *possibly* benefit from counseling....or with time, *accept* the fact that the relationship is over? This is a *judgment* call on your part which may require the *assistance* of a skilled counselor.

SUPERVISED VISITS

Depending upon the circumstances, visits with the abusive parent may need to be conducted under *supervision*. The more violence-prone the visiting parent, the more appropriate the need for such a court-ordered program.

The distinct possibility of committing the *ultimate* revenge.... the killing of one's own child....cannot be taken lightly with *some* offenders.

A supervised visitation center, properly staffed and equipped, might provide a reasonable level of safety for the victim and child.

In *addition* to monitoring visits, on-site counseling programs and seminars could be *incorporated* into the overall operation of the facility. Special emphasis should be placed on safety, security, comfort and educational opportunity for all participants.

UNSUPERVISED VISITS

The multitude of conflicting feelings and emotions toward the visiting parent must be *anticipated* and dealt with.

The issue of unsupervised visitation should be *preceded* with adequate, realistic, age-appropriate *planning*....aided by a professional counselor *if* required....but always in *consultation* with the non-abusing parent.

Unsupervised visits can help children begin to *manage* fear and anxiety, develop safety *skills* and formulate realistic safety *plans* in order to *minimize* the risk of violence during the visitation.

IMPROPER USE OF CHILDREN

Within the context of a visitation arrangement, children should *not:*

▶ Be requested or allowed to *mediate* or *referee* any debate between the parents.

▶ Be used to *spy* on their mother and *report* on her activities.

▶ Be used as *intermediaries* to coax their mother into allowing the father to come back home.

CHILDREN CAN WIN OR LOSE

The success or failure of the visitation process depends to a large degree upon the attitude and intentions of the visiting parent. If such parent truly *cares* for the child and is able to so *demonstrate*, the chances for success are vastly improved.

If on the other hand the parent is not genuinely concerned with the health and well-being of the child or uses the child as a means to terrorize, antagonize or manipulate the mother, such parent-child relationship is severely *jeopardized.*

It must be remembered that children are neither punching bags nor bodyguards. Their mission is to stay safe....not protect the parent to the point where their own safety is endangered.

Part 6 - C

RECUPERATION

T his final segment of the Domestic Violence Survival Guide will address two aspects of recuperation: the **abuser's** (in brief recap format highlighting *rehabilitation*) and the **victim's** (a succinct discussion of the topic highlighting *recovery*).

VICTIM'S RECUPERATION

You are now at the *final* stage in your long, arduous confrontation with domestic violence. Let us assume that you have safely terminated the relationship. He's finally gone. He's out of your life. It's over! But now what?

THE ROAD TO RECOVERY

Just as you would require *healing* and *therapy* following a serious medical ailment, so must you now *recuperate* with special *care* and *attention* to relieve you from (what may have been years of) emotional trauma brought about by the turmoil in your relationship.

Recovery is a painful but *necessary* process which can bring about a great sense of inner peace and personal freedom. This process however, should *not* be tackled alone. Few people traumatized by repeated acts of violence can properly diagnose the symptoms, adequately assess the damage, effectively analyze the options and competently prescribe the cure.

DOWN-LOADING

1. Accept the fact that no one deserves the treatment that you endured.

2. Recognize the *destructive* nature of the past.

3. Leave the past *behind* you.

4. Acknowledge the *need* to heal.

5. Benefit from the knowledge and expertise of a trained professional.

6. Unload the *emotional* baggage in a supportive and caring environment, even though it will most likely generate considerable pain, sorrow and grief. (You may for the *first* time, *fully* realize the extent and horror of the abuse).

PERSONAL INTROSPECTION

You have been burned at least once, but now is the time to heal....both physically and emotionally.

✔ "See yourself" before you attempt to turn yourself around.
✔ Get to *know* yourself.
✔ Uncover your *submerged* personal feelings.
✔ Learn to acknowledge, feel and express your *hidden* emotions.
✔ Elevate your low self-esteem.
✔ Learn to take care of *yourself.*
✔ Begin to "listen" to your body when it "talks" to you (i.e., hungry, full, tired, in pain, etc.).
✔ Reverse *negative* attitudes about yourself and your body.
✔ Discover how to lose your *fear* of intimacy.
✔ Learn to *solve*, not run away from problems.

✔ Find out *why* you were attracted to the abuser and *why* you stayed as long as you did.

✔ Learn how to *manage* your stress.

✔ Learn to express anger in a *productive* way.

INTER-PERSONAL CHALLENGE

Having been hurt once in an inter-personal relationship, you need not shut out the world. Instead, you must now learn to *heal* as a socially functioning human being.

1. Accept the fact that you *deserve* an intimate, mutual and satisfying relationship.

2. Create inter-personal attachments.

3. Learn to *trust* others.

4. Develop *healthy* relationships.

5. Build a *receptiveness* for intimacy.

Self-analysis, best done through a professional therapist, requires that you discover *why* you value yourself so *little* and that you put up with someone who uses and abuses you to such an *extreme*.

ADJUSTMENT PERIOD

Once the abuser is gone....*really* gone out of your life....there will be both *inherent* changes and *necessary* changes to you and your lifestyle.

The expected or *inherent* changes may include facing single parenthood, disrupted family life, financial shortfalls, apprehension, even loneliness.

The *necessary* changes or adjustments might encompass *improvements* to your physical appearance, philosophical outlook, social networking, career enhancement and educational enlightenment. These adjustments should be intended and designed to help create a *better* you....not a different person, but an *improved* version of the original.

By acquiring help through research and reading, lectures and seminars, counseling and therapy, you can hope to make the *necessary* improvements *and* tackle those initially difficult changes which often manifest themselves soon after the separation and termination begins.

As with many of life's endeavors, your keys to *success* are motivation, determination and perseverance.

AVENUES TO TRAVEL

You have a destination to reach and a lot of miles to travel. Here is a list of "stops" to make along the way which require your special attention.

These offerings are but *suggestions* to help you to begin to pull yourself up by your bootstraps. They are *not* a panacea or a foolproof solution to *all* your problems. Nor are *all* suggestions relevant to *all* victims.

Finances permitting, pick and choose those suggestions which may be best suited for you. Items listed herein may help you to think of other pertinent ideas as well.

1. Work on your **ATTITUDE:**

      - ☒ Obtain some *self-help* books.
      - ☒ Sign up for a *self-improvement* course.
      - ☒ Be more *assertive*.
      - ☒ "Signal" your *availability* to others.
      - ☒ Project a *friendly* image.

- Keep *busy*.
- Take in a movie, ball game or concert.
- Do something (legal) that you've always wanted to do but never found the time.

2. Work on your **APPEARANCE:**

- Visit the beauty parlor.
- Get a make-over consultation.
- Have your hair and nails done.
- Get into shape.
- Buy some *stylish* new clothes.

3. Work on your **HORIZONS:**

- Understand that there is life *beyond* your doorstep.
- Visit a library or museum.
- Read a newspaper or magazine.
- Watch *educational* T.V. programs.
- Enroll in an adult education course.
- Learn a foreign language.
- Take educational field trips.
- Do some *stimulating* volunteer work.

4. Work on your **AVAILABILITY:**

- Announce to others your desire to enter the dating world.
- Get *out* of the house more often.
- Keep your eyes and ears *open* to what's going on around you.
- Accept *invitations* to parties and social gatherings.
- Attend singles dances and singles functions.

5. Work on your **CHANCES:**

- Dress *attractively* but modestly.
- Maximize the "new" you but be yourself.
- Be *selective* when accepting dates.
- Avoid frequenting *low* class night spots.
- Stay *away* from places that your "X" frequents.
- Read up on *handling* new relationships.
- Be honest and *demand* honesty in return.

6. Work on your **VULNERABILITY:**

- Profit from your past *experience.*
- Be safety conscious especially when *alone.*
- Project a secure, self-confident image.
- Park your vehicle in *well-lighted* areas.
- Have your keys in hand and *ready* to use.
- Keep your doors *locked* at all times.
- Have a whistle and/or mace *accessible.*
- Remain in *public* when with a stranger.
- Refuse to go to secluded or undesirable locations.
- Minimize your vulnerability for a date/gang rape situation.

7. Work on your **FAMILY:**

- Open a *dialogue* with your children.
- Get their views on "quality" time.
- Arrange a family outing.
- Attempt to make up for any *past* neglect.
- Devote necessary time and attention to their present *needs.*
- Monitor homework and school assignments.
- Review progress reports and report cards.
- Confer with school guidance counselors.

READY FOR LOVE

You have come to the point where you feel the need or desire to date again. This juncture *requires* some forethought.

MAY I HAVE THIS DANCE?

Whether or not and when to resume *dating* is a personal judgment call. Much depends upon the *status* of your *former* relationship. Is he truly out of your life? Has he left town for good? Has he begun a relationship with another woman? Are you reasonably confident that his animosity toward you has significantly subsided?

In other words, is it safe for you to venture out into the dating world? No one can answer that question except you....preferably in consultation with a trained counselor or wise confidant. In any case, you should let time pass but keep *busy.*

It may be advisable to *discreetly* gauge his behavior *before* you resume dating. What is he up to? What does he do on his nights and weekends off? Is he out socializing or is he laying low waiting for you to make your move?

By all means, do not let him know that you are showing *any* interest, curiosity or concern about him. It could be *misinterpreted* as a desire on your part to reconcile.

LOOK BEFORE LEAPING

Rather than falling into the same old trap when venturing into what is sometimes cynically referred to as the "meat market" of dating, *study* up on relationships and the dynamics of inter-personal alliances beforehand.

Do some *research* on human *nature* in general and human *behavioral* traits of the opposite sex in particular.

If you've been burned more than once, take a *course* on personality and character disorders. A basic psychology course can open avenues of information to help you better assess your prospective partners.

While you're in a learning mode, *read* up on assertiveness training for yourself. If *he's* assertive and you're *not,* you are at a distinct *disadvantage* in the relationship.

LEARN FROM YOUR EXPERIENCE

You've been through a traumatic experience. Do not *waste* the knowledge which you have gained by gravitating toward *another* abusive individual. Instead, do yourself, your children, your family and all those who love and care about you a favor. Put your new-found ability to *recognize* abusive types to good use. Pick them out and cast them aside.

Keep going....keep looking....keep thinking....keep remembering. Maintain your dignity and self-respect. Be yourself. Be good to yourself. Be selective. Be honest and forthright. Be determined to succeed. Be prepared to survive.

DATING "ADVANTAGES"

Patterns of power and control *can* become evident *before* marriage or co-habitation. The union need not be "legal" nor consummated for negative signs to emerge in the relationship.

On the plus side, early-on, dating relationships usually lack the legal, financial, property and custody entanglements common to people who are married, live together or have a child in common.

This *should* facilitate the termination process. The longer you wait, the more time the abuser has to exert his superficial charm and manipulate the relationship until he's got you where he wants you....under his influence and control.

WHICH DIRECTION TO GO?

You've decided that you are ready, willing and able to begin dating....and hopefully find a suitable companion or partner. So now what?

■ **"ADVERTISE" YOURSELF** - It often pays to *announce*....to let your friends, family and co-workers know that you want to get out and meet someone special. But *before* you start looking for a *particular* individual, try to meet a variety of people. Get to know *different* people from *different* backgrounds.

You'll begin to realize that the "problem personality" is not the only personality. Not all men are like him. Not all men are to be feared. There are honest, decent, respectable, substance-free men out there.

To meet them you must socialize and mingle; join groups for single parents, attend meetings, go to public gatherings and become active in local civic groups. You'll have to work at it. Dating is a bit like a second job but make the most of it.

■ **DATING SERVICES** - Commercially operated, computer-assisted dating services have helped many people over the years. This being so, they may possibly help you. But *before* signing up with any such service, do your *homework*.

Check for any complaints with the Better Business Bureau and the Department of Consumer Affairs or its local equivalent. Check the competition. Check for references. Make sure you can *cancel* if you're not satisfied.

Ascertain if they utilize, and to what extent they employ, an application investigation and screening process. Such a procedure, aimed at weeding out *undesirable* applicants, can work to your best interests....saving you time and possibly trouble.

Other than that, think positive, put your best effort into the program and as always, be *cautious*....using your recognition skills and your *determination* to put the brakes on *any* relationship that doesn't look or feel right.

■ **PERSONALS** - Generally speaking, personal ads in newspapers, magazines and periodicals have lost the stigma   which was prevalent when they first appeared. Today, many professional and para-professional people utilize this method for meeting others.

Nurses, teachers, business people, even police officers have been known to place and answer these ads. Often busy with their personal and professional lives, they cannot easily devote the time required to do social expeditions.

As with any encounter with a *stranger*....whether by chance meeting, blind date, personal ad, dating service or cyberspace introduction....*caution* is imperative.

Personal information should never be divulged at the outset. Initial meetings should take place in very *public* places such as a restaurant, coffee shop or crowded park.

Separate transportation is essential. After your meeting, you must make sure you are not being *followed* home.

If you come to the point where you wish to see this person again, ask for his *home* phone number. This tactic should help prevent getting involved with a married or co-habitating individual.

As with any budding relationship, go slow, keep your eyes and ears open and make mental notes of any negative or suspicious behavior. If the vibes are *bad,* put an *end* to it.

AVOID NOW; BENEFIT LATER

In the beginning, increasing your social circle and your dating *options* is usually more important than focusing your energies on *one* individual. It is therefore best to:

☒ Avoid *rushing* to meet a *permanent* mate.

☒ Avoid *peer* pressure to find someone fast.

☒ Avoid making the best of a *mediocre* relationship in order to please *others*.

☒ Avoid self-deception; be realistic when *assessing* the potential for happiness (or trouble).

☒ Avoid any temptation to *ignore* the warning signs of impending or potential danger.

☒ Avoid *rationalizing* a bad situation to make it *appear* better.

DISCOVERY PROCESS

You've found someone that you're interested in. Now you need to find out about him. Actually, you *must* find out about him. You must discover if there are any *skeletons* in his closet.

Casual conversations should be directed towards uncovering as much information about your new friend as is reasonably possible.

Where he works is less important (assuming that it's a legal occupation) than what he does *after* work. Your mission is to discover his interests, his hobbies and his recreational pursuits.

What about his friends? What are they like? Do they seem okay? If they are loud, obnoxious brutes, beware!

Is he up on current events, or is *he* the center of his own little world? Must he get intoxicated in order to have a good time or has he used or suggested the use of drugs in order to better enjoy the evening?

Does he brag about the use of physical force against former wives or girl friends? Does his body language reveal a duplicitous nature? Has your internal warning mechanism triggered an ALERT as yet?

WHAT'S HIS REPUTATION ?

You've asked around, right? After all, if he's bad news, you don't want to be the *last* to know.

If you discover that he has an unsavory reputation.... especially a propensity for serious, anti-social and deeply-ingrained habits....don't operate under the assumption that *you* can change him. "He'll be different with me," you may say. But *don't* count on it!

If he's known around town as "a real ladies' man," do you simply want to be just another stepping stone on the path to his hedonistic heaven?

If he is known to get "a bit obnoxious" *only* when he drinks too much, what is their *definition* of obnoxious and how *often* does he get loaded?

WHAT YOU SEE IS WHAT YOU GET ?

Most people present their *best* image on the first date and in the early stages of a dating relationship. This *could* be the best it will *ever* be. In time, the "real" personality and character may emerge from behind the false and temporary facade.

Can you be fooled into believing his statements and apparent sincerity? Of course....especially by someone who has had years of practice and experience.

But once you've "unmasked" him, you must essentially accept him as he is *or* go on to the next available prospect. Your chances of changing him to coincide with your expectations are slim to none. Besides being a waste of time, your efforts might invite danger.

If his "best" is bad, imagine how uncomfortable you'll feel....and vulnerable you may become....when he displays his *worst*. Early warning signs *must* be heeded!

EVALUATION PROCESS

From the *moment* the relationship *begins* (introduction, conversation, phone chats, first date, etc.) you must initiate the evaluation process. The *ultimate* goal may be to determine if your new acquaintance is a "good catch" but your *initial* objective is to discover whether he is decent and trustworthy.

In essence, you must "see where he's coming from" and ascertain why he is interested in *you.* Since your personal safety may be at risk, you must hone your intuitive and investigative skills in order to make an accurate appraisal.

In the very early stage of the relationship you must rely on observation and instinct. If the dating continues, inquiry and investigation, both subtle and direct, can help to answer the following important questions:

1. Is he *truthful* about himself?
2. Is he able to *communicate* his true feelings?
3. Is he what you expected?
4. Is he truly romantic or just over-sexed?
5. Is he *emotionally* stable?
6. Is he *capable* of committing to another?
7. And finally, is he *really* your type or are you fascinated by his off-beat behavior?

GET A SECOND OPINION

Since your assessment of Mr. Wonderful may be too *subjective,* use a wise and trusted friend as a sounding board.

Tell her everything you know about him thus far. Describe your first few dates as though you were giving a report.

Then evaluate *her* objective, unbiased opinion. She may very well see some warning signs that you have overlooked.

If however, you've reached the point where you believe that Mr. W. is the *most* important person in your life and that *he* knows you *better* than your family and friends do, then you will probably *ignore* their otherwise valued opinions and suggestions. This would likely be a mistake.

FIRST DATE = FIRST OPPORTUNITY

One of the best ways to evaluate your new dating partner is to watch him *interact* with others. This effectively *excludes* a movie, a walk in the park or a drive in the country. In these settings, he can virtually monopolize the conversation and control the direction of the date.

A dinner date at a nice restaurant on the other hand, provides an excellent opportunity to check out his "people skills" (as well as his dining and hygiene habits).

Does he, for example, treat you special *but* treat the valet, the coat-check girl or the hostess in a subservient manner? Is he pleasant with you *but* rude to the waitress?

If he seems nice to you but nasty to others, interpret that as a "red flag." If he's two-faced now, expect dual treatment later....next time at *your* expense.

VIGILANCE PAYS

Be vigilant. Be alert. Be observant. Be strong. Your personal goal must mesh with society's: a steadfast *intolerance* of any form of domestic abuse or violence.

- ☉ Confront your feelings and your abusive past in order to develop a healthy and satisfying relationship.
- ☉ Is he a dormant volcano, camouflaged with compliments and flowers? Effective *recognition* must activate a built-in *prevention* mechanism.
- ☉ The sooner you *retreat* from this new and tempting but foreboding and unsettling relationship, the sooner you can *avoid* problems....maybe even disaster.
- ☉ Be grateful if you *know* that you are choosing "lemons." This places you in a better position to *do* something about it.
- ☉ Resist slipping backwards into the familiar pattern of *accepting* abuse, then *denying* that it is recurring or *minimizing* the potential for danger.
- ☉ Repeating such patterns can be caused by an *inability* to imagine an *alternative*.
- ☉ If a warm, positive relationship surfaces, you may not know how to deal with it because it seems too alien to you based on your *limited* knowledge of inter-personal relationships. This somewhat deep-seated psychological drawback calls for professional *counseling*.
- ☉ Be ever mindful that AIDS and sexually transmitted diseases are still very much with us.

THE "LITTLE WHITE LIE"

Understand that some people *do* lie or grossly exaggerate stories about themselves. Why? In order to sound important, impress their listener, gain sympathy, conceal the truth or support previously told lies.

Beware the pathological liar who must overstate or embellish nearly everything he says. His life is a facade. He becomes an actor and you are his audience. You must therefore learn to *critique* his "performance," separate the superficial persona, distinguish fantasy from reality and be ready to give him a *bad* review.

DON'T BE A POLLYANNA

You must be *realistic*, especially if you've led a sheltered life. There *are,* in varying degrees, demented, mischievous, bad and evil people in the world. They *do* exist and *may* be found in any given community.

Not all sex offenders have been apprehended. Not all criminals are behind bars. Not all mentally ill people are in institutions.

Many criminal types are looking for their *first* victim. Thanks to flaws in the criminal justice system, many eager and experienced predators have evaded prison or have been released with little time served and are looking for their *next* victim.

Remember, the classic characteristic of a con artist is his special ability to generate *trust* in his victim. His charming persona breaks down any *suspicion* and facilitates his underhanded mission. Many a naive woman brought home a "nice guy" after a brief introduction, only to be assaulted, raped or murdered.

You must, therefore, work with *maximum* effort to avoid and evade the grip of a duplicitous suitor.

PRACTICE MAKES PERFECT

Repetition at the dating game should increase proficiency in *assessing* new prospects, *discovering* their inadequacies, *evaluating* their potential and *confronting* real or imagined problems.

This increased proficiency should yield greater self-confidence and subsequently the freedom and ability to make *wiser* choices down the road.

As an *active* participant in the process, you must learn to put the "weeding out" procedure to good and effective use.

Carefully calculated, the +'s and -'s of your final selection should equal the sum total of your partner....be he friend or foe, lover or leaver, saint or sinner, amorous or abusive.

It can be your choice!

SPECIAL WARNING

If you are re-entering the dating scene after a recent divorce or separation which was less than amicable....and *especially* if there is an active Order of Protection in effect against your "ex".... and more *especially* if he continues to believe that you still "belong" to him....be up front and honest with your new acquaintance about your domestic history.

To flaunt a new partner in front of your old partner in public is one thing. But to bring him into "his house" ....and worse, into "his bed".... too soon, is inviting *catastrophe.*

You may have legal *right* to do so but you also have a legal right to engage in any number of dangerous, imprudent acts. Does that mean you should? Common sense should always prevail....especially if you have children residing in the house with you who stand to be *further* traumatized if your former partner *confronts* you and your new houseguest in the middle of the night.

HELPING OTHERS

Because of the ordeal which you were subjected to, you are now in a sense, a quasi-expert on the subject of dealing with and surviving domestic violence.

Armed with this fund of knowledge and experience, you may be able to help another person by providing meaningful support....helping to take her out of the valley of victimization and into the sunlight of **SURVIVAL.**

❑ Be on the lookout for *symptoms* of domestic violence in friends, family members, co-workers, or even neighbors.

❑ Be *prepared* to offer help or referral....directly, indirectly or even anonymously.

❑ Offer your *assistance* to someone you know to be or suspect to be in an abusive relationship.

❑ Be direct, but gentle.

❑ Encourage discussion.

❑ Demonstrate your interest and concern.

❑ Listen without pressing for details.

❑ Allow *time* for full answers and the venting of pent-up feelings.

❑ Avoid challenging her version of the incident.

❑ Respect the need for confidentiality.

❑ Avoid being judgmental.

❑ Inform her that her situation is not an isolated case.

❑ Assure her that she is not to blame.

❑ Inform her that violence is a *crime* and is *never* justifiable.

❏ Tell her that apologies and promises alone will not end the violence.

❏ Advise her that the situation will probably get *worse.*

❏ In general, refrain from interceding on her behalf with the batterer.

❏ Avoid quick, easy solutions.

❏ Make a list of community resources and support services.

❏ Discuss the various options.

❏ Share your own survival strategies.

❏ Project a positive, can-do image for added inspiration.

❏ Aid her with a plan to leave safely if that is *her* choice.

❏ Do not force her to leave if she is not ready.

❏ Avoid giving her "instructions" such as when to leave or whether to stay or to attempt a reconciliation.

❏ Allow reasonable time for her to make her own decisions.

❏ If possible, accompany her to the police station and/or hospital, if necessary.

❏ Help her to locate a shelter and whatever support services she may need.

❏ Encourage her to get professional help.

❏ Avoid withdrawing your support if she is not quite ready to enact major changes in her life.

GOING BEYOND BASIC HELP

Suppose that you want to do *more* to help alleviate domestic violence in your community?

FIRST THE BASICS

Even persons who don't care to "get involved" can "be there" for a neighbor or acquaintance in domestic distress. Merely calling for emergency police or medical intervention, when required, can be of significant value.

Help can also be proffered anonymously or through an intermediary. Informing the victim of the location of a women's shelter can be but one small step toward ending her misery. Communicating with the local victim's hotline may provide valuable suggestions regarding the availability of assistance.

Having reason to believe that children are being abused or maltreated in the home would allow the concerned citizen, teacher, babysitter, etc. to notify the child abuse hot line.

Contributing your time or talent in a volunteer capacity to a shelter or community resource center can provide tremendous satisfaction and a sense of accomplishment. Making a monetary contribution to support their operations is another small step in the right direction.

EDUCATE YOURSELF

Any of the following steps can help increase your overall *awareness* on the subject of domestic violence:

1. Learn about anti-violence programs in your community.
2. **Ascertain** the police procedures which apply when responding to a domestic incident.
3. Inquire as to what laws and judicial remedies are available for victims.
4. Ask candidates for elective office to state their platform for preventing and stopping domestic violence.

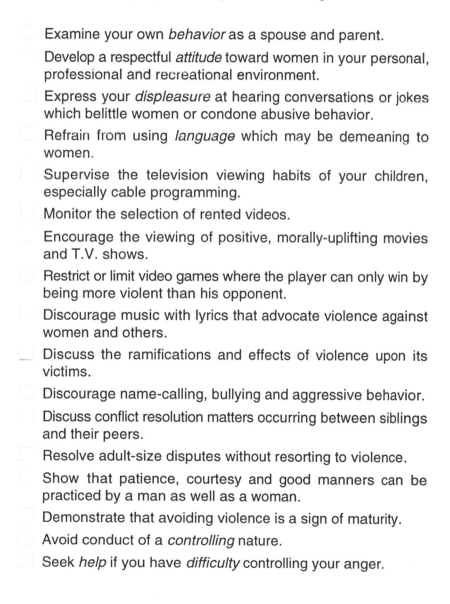

SET A GOOD EXAMPLE

Everyone, regardless of their marital or social status, can become a positive role model in their home, workplace or community-at-large by adhering to the following:

Examine your own *behavior* as a spouse and parent.

Develop a respectful *attitude* toward women in your personal, professional and recreational environment.

Express your *displeasure* at hearing conversations or jokes which belittle women or condone abusive behavior.

Refrain from using *language* which may be demeaning to women.

Supervise the television viewing habits of your children, especially cable programming.

Monitor the selection of rented videos.

Encourage the viewing of positive, morally-uplifting movies and T.V. shows.

Restrict or limit video games where the player can only win by being more violent than his opponent.

Discourage music with lyrics that advocate violence against women and others.

Discuss the ramifications and effects of violence upon its victims.

Discourage name-calling, bullying and aggressive behavior.

Discuss conflict resolution matters occurring between siblings and their peers.

Resolve adult-size disputes without resorting to violence.

Show that patience, courtesy and good manners can be practiced by a man as well as a woman.

Demonstrate that avoiding violence is a sign of maturity.

Avoid conduct of a *controlling* nature.

Seek *help* if you have *difficulty* controlling your anger.

- Demonstrate moderation in the use of alcoholic beverages.
- Forbid the presence of any drugs in the home.
- Safeguard any firearm lawfully kept in the home.
- Dispose of any unlicensed, unwanted or unneeded firearms in the house.

PARENTS BEWARE !

You may presently maintain a violence-free home but can unknowingly be raising *future* domestic abusers. If your teenagers are overly *aggressive* in settling disputes with others or putting their acquaintances "in their place," you should nip these tendencies in the bud *before* they become ingrained in their day-to-day habits. Macho behavior....the "cool" way to handle a grudge or grievance....can land Mr. Hotshot in a legal hot-seat.

So beware parents! Attorney's fees, court costs, fines, restitution, lost wages, medical bills and the like, will result in an all-for-one out-of-control fist landing upon someone who *didn't* even "deserve" it.

It is far better....and more practical....for parents to *instill* respect for others, respect for themselves and respect for the law, in their children, than to risk the consequences of civil and criminal liability under such laws.

PROBING CHILDREN FOR ANSWERS   " ? "

Children *residing* in a violent home are *hurting* in more ways than one. Though they may not be the *intended* victims, emotional trauma is a given, and accidental injury is a distinct possibility. Even if they are not being physically harmed themselves, the psychological harm can take a tremendous *toll* over time.

Many such children suffer from guilt, shame and embarrassment. Discussing what goes on in the house is apt to be minimized or avoided entirely.

If you suspect or have reason to believe that a child is struggling to cope with a *violent* family life, you should make a concerted effort to open a line of communication because these young, virtually *helpless* victims desperately want to get *relief* and *stability* in their lives.

In pursuing this goal, the following steps may prove beneficial:

- Be *gentle* in your overall approach.
- Be *direct* if possible, taking age and level of maturity into account.
- If the direct approach is not feasible, discuss the matter in *general* terms or by means of a *hypothetical* family.
- Seek to establish a level of *trust* and *confidence* between yourself and the child.
- Express your interest and concern.
- Assure the child that there are *adults* around who care.
- Be a good listener.
- Empathize with the *difficulty* of the situation.
- Inform the child that he is *not* responsible for what is taking place within the home.
- Tell the child that violence is *never* okay.
- Contact the appropriate agency to *report* physical or sexual abuse, if so discovered.
- Be *available*, if the child chooses to seek you out upon further developments in the home.

CONFRONTING THE AGGRESSOR

Bringing up the subject of domestic violence with someone who you suspect or believe to be a violator can be an unpleasant assignment. Sometimes however, it may be *necessary* to get the issue out in the open.

When faced with the need or advisability to confront such issues, you might want to consider the following:

- Seek to *confirm* your suspicions through personal observation, consensus with others or some other independent means.
- Engage in a *dialogue* concerning the relationship.
- Note any *admissions* of abuse or controlling tactics.
- Take the opportunity to cast a negative or disapproving view of such behavior.
- Express your point of view despite any *denial* of abuse or violence.
- Relate the personal, legal, financial and social *consequences* of domestic violence.
- Advise him of the detrimental effects upon any *children* or other *family* members.
- Impress upon him that you are concerned with the safety and well-being of *all* those who reside within the home.
- Inform him that violence can *not* be tolerated by anyone.
- Inform him that *help* is available and that the situation will probably get *worse* without it.
- Urge him to solicit such help.
- Continue *monitoring* the situation, especially if faced with repeated denials.

BECOME AN ACTIVIST

If you are inclined to take a more *active* role in the campaign against domestic violence, the following suggestions may be helpful:

■ Engage government, law enforcement, judicial, prosecution, health, social services, religious, civic and educational entities to *join* in a community coalition to study, assess and end the violence.

■ Present fact-finding studies and reports to federal, state and local legislative committees.

■ Join, support and contribute to a state-wide or national coalition against domestic violence.

■ Work with your local domestic violence coalition on community education, assistance and legislative initiatives.

■ Organize local chapter to help raise awareness about domestic violence.

■ Campaign *for* women's safety and *against* abusive behavior at your place of employment and recreation.

■ Form a discussion group in your social, fraternal or religious organization.

■ Solicit volunteers within your organization to provide cooking, babysitting, reading, typing or other needed services at a local domestic violence shelter.

■ Suggest that your business, professional or civic organization "adopts" a local shelter with financial support.

■ Invite representatives of your local Criminal Justice System, women's shelter and support services to address your meetings.

■ Address local civic groups and community associations if *you* are well versed on the topic of recognition, prevention and survival of domestic violence.

■ Form a citizen's group to monitor and gauge the effectiveness of the local domestic violence programs.

■ Petition your legislators to support and enact effective anti-violence legislation.

■ Encourage local police to authorize and organize a weapons buy back, turn-in or amnesty program.

■ Suggest, encourage or support innovative and experimental police-community cooperative efforts such as a volunteer "ride-along" program....or help perfect and expand existing programs which increase public awareness and offer on-scene support to the victim.

■ Voice your opinion on the issue of violence against women to television, radio, recording and motion picture executives.

■ Notify advertisers and boycott products which sponsor negative messages in the print, communication and entertainment media.

■ Promote community projects which heighten awareness about violence in the home.

◘ Encourage youth groups to get out the message that *hitting* another person is wrong and *tolerating* being hit is wrong as well.

◘ Work with P.T.A. groups to educate school age children on what a *healthy* relationship is, what *constitutes* abuse and how to *peacefully* resolve conflicts.

◘ Help distribute anti-violence literature and posters at select locations in the community, *preferably* where women are more apt to notice them, such as supermarkets, laundromats, hair salons, gyms, libraries, restrooms, doctor's waiting rooms, schools, etc.

◘ Petition local government leaders to establish a "panic alarm" program whereby remote controlled devices are supplied to victims facing an on-going threat of continued violence. Participants should have a *current* Order of Protection in effect and agree in advance to cooperate in the prosecution process.

◘ Sponsor a no cost, cellular phone loaner program for an *eligible* victim in your community. Such phones can be *programmed* to dial 9-1-1 *only*. Criteria for eligibility can include: the victim being a local resident, her not *residing* with the abuser, a serious charge involved, agreement to cooperate with authorities, a court order in effect, a court case pending, children at risk, extenuating circumstances, etc.

This page intentionally left blank.

Conclusion

DOMESTIC VIOLENCE SURVIVAL GUIDE

You have met the monster we call Domestic Violence and traveled through the belly of the beast.

You have learned about abuse, what constitutes unlawful acts upon you, how to seek help, how to help yourself, how to seek protection, how to operate within the criminal justice system, how to go about repairing a repairable relationship or how to end a bad one, and finally, how to get yourself back on track and in control of your life.

In retrospect, we believe that the two most *vital* portions of this publication are Recognition and Prevention. Young adults entering the dating world....even teenagers forming new relationships....must learn to *recognize* the violence-prone companion or person with abusive tendencies or inclinations.

Just as any intelligent person who recognizes a volcano will *avoid* stepping near the rim, people in new relationships must *retreat* from those with hot temperaments or volatile personalities....the sooner the better!

If you are fortunate enough to have survived an abusive or violent relationship, your best assurance to survive *another* one is to *see* it coming and *evade* it before it seizes you again.

The *early* recognition and prevention strategies are your *best* hope for *continued* survival against domestic abuse and violence.

At the risk of sounding pessimistic, a dose of *reality* is in order, lest you be misled into a *false* sense of security.

As the traditional two-parent family structure continues to decline, as morals and mores continue to erode, as the quality of life continues to descend and as crime and violence becomes commonplace in our society, the number of domestic violence cases will undoubtedly *increase.*

But unfortunately, there is no *fool-proof* strategy yet devised to *guarantee* against domestic abuse or violence. There are *no* guarantees when it comes to the need to feel secure from the aggression of a past or present partner.

No single person, government agency or legal entity can prevent or terminate this scourge upon society and the family.

A judge's verbal admonition against violence will not prevent violence. A duly signed and served order of protection is not a guarantee against an assault. Counseling and therapy can not guarantee the desired results. Even around the clock police protection is not an assurance against attack.

An enraged, irrational or psychotic person can....barring an indefinite incarceration....land an attack upon his victim.

Ironically, what would seem to be a most secure environment, a court house....with police officers, bailiffs and security personnel on hand....is often a magnet for anger, hostility and vengeance.

Only through personal awareness, initiative and resolve can the victim of domestic violence *begin* to tame the monster.

Only through the dedicated efforts of the criminal justice system and intervention specialists can the victim   battle successfully and survive.

Fortunately, national concern and public awareness is on the rise. Louder and more numerous voices are calling for tougher legislation to protect the abused, punish the abuser and provide meaningful counseling and therapy for both.

Also responding to public concern, the criminal justice system has been put on notice that inaction and indifference are inappropriate! Expectations are higher and increasingly improved results are anticipated.

It is our sincere hope that this publication has opened your eyes and your mind to the problem of, handling of and **survival** of relationship abuse and domestic violence.

Any comments or suggestions that you may have, relative to this topic, will be read with interest and appreciation.

Attention:

NEW YORK STATE RESIDENTS

The **New York State Edition**...a specially edited version of the *Domestic Violence Survival Guide* incorporating applicable portions of the New York State:

- **Penal Law**
- **Family Court Act**
- **Criminal Procedure Law**

including the **Civil Rights Law** and **Mental Hygiene Law**, with reference and resource listings from the **Domestic Relations Law** and **Social Services Law.**

In addition to the general information contained in our regular edition, the New York State edition places special emphasis on the following areas for victims of relationship abuse and domestic violence:

- **Legal Issues**
- **Family Court Matters**
- **Criminal Law and Proceedings**
- **Court Jurisdiction and Procedures**

A thought-provoking, option-packed guide on how to

Recognize, Prevent, Terminate and Survive

an encounter with

Relationship Abuse and Domestic Violence

Offers a crash course on self-preservation
A Must-Have for:
Victims of abuse and their loved ones, Criminal Justice personnel, social service workers, and all those who may be called upon to act as counsellors.

Contains a new and unique approach to an old and confounding problem and is packed with positive, time-tested tactics and new strategies for survival.

Please send _____ copy(ies) of **The New York State Domestic Violence Survival Guide** (Looseleaf Edition - 5 1/2 x 8 ½ Over 300 pages), at a cost of **$24.95** per copy plus postage & handling and sales tax. This is a pre-publication notice, anticipated availability Fall 1996.

PLEASE PRINT CLEARLY

_____
Name

_____
Street Address   **Apt. No.**

_____
Town & State   **Zip Code**

Daytime Phone Number (_____)_____

Telephone Orders by Credit Card or UPS-COD:
(800) 647-5547

Postage & Handling (*INSURED*)
($4.00 for the first item, plus $3.00 for the
second item and $2.00 for each item thereafter. $_____
Items under $6.00, $2.50 each.)

Optional First Class ($2.00 extra per order) $_____

Sales Tax _____% $_____

AMOUNT DUE: $_____

Credit Card #:_____
(M.C./Visa/AMEX/Discover)   (Exp. Date)

LOOSELEAF LAW PUBLICATIONS, INC.
P.O. Box 650042, Fresh Meadows, N.Y. 11365-0042
Telephone: (718) 359-5559
also **24 Hour Fax No. (718) 539-0941**
Place order by phone 9-5, M-F EST

Bibliography

DOMESTIC VIOLENCE SURVIVAL GUIDE

Suggested Readings for:

VICTIMS IN GENERAL

❑ **The Battered Woman**
by Lenore Walker
Harper and Row; New York, NY (1982)

❑ **Women and Male Violence**
by Susan Schechter
South End Press; Boston, MA (1983)

❑ **Getting Free: You Can End Abuse and Take Back Your Life**
by Ginny NiCarthy
Seal Press; Seattle, WA (1986)

❑ **Next Time She'll Be Dead: Battering and How to Stop It**
by Ann Jones
Beacon Press; Boston, MA (1994)

❑ **Don't Let Him Hurt Me Anymore: A Self-Help Guide for Women in Abusive Relationships**
by Alexis Asher
Burning Gate Press; Tarzana, CA (1994)

❑ **Men Who Batter: An Integrated Approach to Stopping Wife Abuse**
by Edward Gondolf
Learning Publications; Holmes Beach, FL (1985)

❑ **When Love Goes Wrong: What to Do When You Can't Do Anything Right**
by Ann Jones and Susan Schechter
Harper Collins; New York, NY (1992)

DATING VICTIMS

❑ **Dating Violence: Young Women In Danger**
by Barrie Levy
Seal Press; Seattle, WA (1991)

CHILD VICTIMS

❑ **Children of Battered Women: Issues in Child Development and Intervention Planning**
by P. Jaffe, S. Wilson and D. W. Wolfe
Sage Publications; Newbury Park, CA (1990)

FAMILY VICTIMS

❑ **Behind Closed Doors: Violence in the American Family**
by M. Straus, R. Gelles and S. Steinmetz
Anchor Books; New York, NY (1977)

PREGNANT VICTIMS

❑ **Prevention of Battering During Pregnancy: Focus on Behavioral Change**
by A. Helton, J. McFarlane and E. Anderson
Public Health Nursing; Vol. 4, Sept. (1987)

SENIOR VICTIMS

❑ **Role of the Criminal Justice System in Elder Abuse Cases**
by Candace Heisler
Journal of Elder Abuse and Neglect; Vol. 3 (1991)

GAY VICTIMS

❑ **Men Who Beat the Men Who Love Them: Battered Gay Men and Domestic Violence**
by David Island and Patrick Letellier
Haworth Press; Binghamton, NY (1991)

LESBIAN VICTIMS

❑ **Naming The Violence: Speaking Out About Lesbian Battering**
Kerry Lobel, Editor
Seal Press; Seattle, WA (1986)

IMMIGRANT VICTIMS

❑ **Domestic Violence in Immigrant and Refugee Communities**
by Family Violence Prevention Fund
San Francisco, CA (1991)

HISPANIC VICTIMS

❑ **Mejor Sola Que Mal Acompanada: For The Latina In An Abusive Relationship**
by Myrna Zambrano
Seal Press; Seattle, WA (1985)

WOMEN OF COLOR

❑ **Chain, Chain, Change: For Black Women Dealing With Physical and Emotional Abuse**
by Evelyn White
Seal Press; Seattle, WA (1985)

This page intentionally left blank.

Nationwide Resources

DOMESTIC VIOLENCE SURVIVAL GUIDE

One or more of the following organizations should be contacted by victims and advocacy groups for **guidance** on networking and referrals, activities and agendas, training and planning; **information** on membership and funding, programs and services, seminars and workshops; **sources** for newsletters and bulletins, visual aids and posters, products and publications.

Note that the telephone numbers listed herein are *not* for crisis intervention. Always dial 9-1-1 in emergencies and hot-lines for immediate support.

◻ **National Resource Center on Domestic Violence**
6400 Flank Drive (Suite 1300)
Harrisburg, PA 17112
800/537-2238

◻ **Resource Center on Domestic Violence, Child Protection and Custody** (c/o N.C.J.F.C.J)
P.O. Box 8970
Reno, NV 89507
800/527-3223

◻ **Battered Women's Justice Project**
4032 Chicago Avenue
Minneapolis, MN 55407
800/903-0111

◻ **National Coalition Against Domestic Violence**
P.O. Box 18749
Denver, CO 80218
303/839-1852

◻ **National Network to End Domestic Violence**
8701 N. Mopac Expressway (Suite 450)
Austin, TX 78759
512/794-1133

- **Family Violence Prevention Fund**
383 Rhode Island Street (Suite 304)
San Francisco, CA 94103
415/252-8900

- **National Crime Prevention Council**
1700 K Street NW
Washington, DC 20006
202/466-6272

Internet Web Pages

DOMESTIC VIOLENCE SURVIVAL GUIDE

THE WORLDWIDE WEB has waves of women-oriented sites available for those who are able to venture out to surf.

◎ For an excellent launching point, with a keyboard search function and a set of topics to be browsed:

http://www.femina.com

◎ *cybergrrl* provides another good launch point for women's issues available via cyber technology:

http://www.cybergrrl.com/cg.htm/

◎ For on-line computer access to pertinent laws, phone numbers, resources, etc. dealing with domestic violence.

http://www.usdoj.gov/vawo

◎ Articles, news stories and feedback forums are available plus advice columns on relationships, careers, personal finance and more:

http://www.women.com

◎ Access over 1,000 different national and international self-help groups, including information and support for abused women, alcoholism, parental matters, etc.

http://www.cmhc.com/selfhelp/

◉ From *Divorce Magazine*, billed as the only publication for the divorced and divorcing, this medium is now on the Internet as well as the printed page:

http://www.divorcemag.com/divorce

◉ The National Organization for Women, prominent advocacy group in the forefront of women's rights and women's issues, can be reached via the Internet:

http://now.org/now/home.htm/

DOMESTIC VIOLENCE SURVIVAL GUIDE

INDEX

INDEX